Catholicism: A Very Short Introduction

VERY SHORT INTRODUCTIONS are for anyone wanting a stimulating and accessible way in to a new subject. They are written by experts, and have been published in more than 25 languages worldwide.

The series began in 1995, and now represents a wide variety of topics in history, philosophy, religion, science, and the humanities. Over the next few years it will grow to a library of around 200 volumes – a Very Short Introduction to everything from ancient Egypt and Indian philosophy to conceptual art and cosmology.

For more information visit our websites
www.oup.com/uk/vsi
www.oup.com/us

Gerald O'Collins

CATHOLICISM

A Very Short Introduction

OXFORD
UNIVERSITY PRESS

OXFORD
UNIVERSITY PRESS

Great Clarendon Street, Oxford OX2 6DP

Oxford University Press is a department of the University of Oxford.
It furthers the University's objective of excellence in research, scholarship,
and education by publishing worldwide in

Oxford New York

Auckland Cape Town Dar es Salaam Hong Kong Karachi
Kuala Lumpur Madrid Melbourne Mexico City Nairobi
New Delhi Shanghai Taipei Toronto

With offices in

Argentina Austria Brazil Chile Czech Republic France Greece
Guatemala Hungary Italy Japan Poland Portugal Singapore
South Korea Switzerland Thailand Turkey Ukraine Vietnam

Oxford is a registered trade mark of Oxford University Press
in the UK and in certain other countries

Published in the United States
by Oxford University Press Inc., New York

British Library Cataloguing in Publication Data

Data available

Library of Congress Cataloging in Publication Data

O'Collins, Gerald.
Catholicism : a very short introduction / Gerald O'Collins.
p. cm. – (Very short introductions)
Includes index.
ISBN 978-0-19-954591-9
1. Catholic Church–Doctrines.
2. Catholic Church–Customs and practices. I. Title.
BX1754.O23 2008
282-dc22   2008031677

ISBN 978-0-19-954591-9

1 3 5 7 9 10 8 6 4 2

Typeset by SPI Publisher Services, Pondicherry, India
Printed in Great Britain by
Ashford Colour Press Ltd, Gosport, Hampshire

Contents

Preface

On 8 April 2005, up to three billion people around the globe watched the televised funeral of John Paul II (pope 1978–2005). They saw many of the distinctive features of the Catholic Church on display as the service for the dead pope was celebrated in front of Saint Peter's Basilica, the largest Christian church in the world.

Lifted high above the crowd like a Viking king, the body of John Paul II had been carried in an open coffin from the Vatican palace, through Saint Peter's Square, and into the basilica. For four days he lay there in state right above the ancient cemetery where Saint Peter was buried after his martyrdom under Emperor Nero. Nearly two million people of different ages, classes in society, and faith convictions filed past to pay their last respects to the dead pope.

After being solemnly closed, the coffin was slowly carried out into the square as the choir chanted the litany of the saints, a prayer that invokes numerous Christian men and women officially recognized for their holiness after their death and that remains very dear to Catholic and Orthodox Christians alike. At the service, rows of cardinals and bishops were gathered near the altar; their red vestments fluttered in the breeze. They were flanked by representatives of Christian churches, ambassadors, prime ministers, presidents, and other heads of state. The crowd

1. Pope John Paul II lies in state in St Peter's Basilica before his funeral on 8 April 2005

of nearly three-quarters of a million stretched beyond the square into the broad Via della Conciliazione and other neighbouring streets. Around the city of Rome several million people followed the funeral on mega-screens.

The funeral service featured many traditional Catholic symbols: the candles guttering in the wind; the smoke of incense rising from thuribles; the book of the Four Gospels opened on his coffin to symbolize the good news by which the dead pope had tried to live; and the holy water sprinkled on his coffin before it was carried away for burial in the crypt of Saint Peter's.

On that spring day in 2005, the television audience around the earth watched the largest and oldest institution in the world burying its dead leader. The global communion of Catholicism was praying for and with the late pope and sharing his passage into eternal life. People everywhere could see for themselves how the Catholic Church 'breathes with two lungs', when first a Western rite deacon and then an Eastern rite deacon sang the Gospel and when, at the end of the ceremony, Eastern rite leaders gathered around the coffin to chant their ancient prayers.

Through television a vast public followed a dramatic moment in the life and practice of Catholics around the world. They could watch and see how the Catholic Church remains vigorous and indisputably important today to Catholics and non-Catholics alike.

'Catholicity' belongs, of course, among the characteristics of the Church confessed by all Christians in the Nicene-Constantinopolitan Creed, a concise version of the chief points of Christian faith that is derived in its full form from the First Council of Constantinople (AD 381). Used at least sometimes every year by all Christians when they celebrate the Eucharist (the sacred rite that commemorates the 'Last Supper' celebrated by Jesus on the night before his death), this Creed declares a common faith in the 'one, holy, *catholic*, and apostolic Church'. This is the confession of many Protestants when they profess the Creed on Sundays, whether or not they meet for the Eucharist. Some people would prefer to give this book the title of *Roman Catholicism*. After all, Catholics are those Christians who are in communion with the bishop of Rome; they accept the universal authority of the pope who lives in the Vatican and presides over the diocese of Rome. Nevertheless, when one speaks or writes of 'Catholics' or 'Catholicism', people almost invariably understand a reference to Roman Catholics. That surely was the presumption behind the invitation to write a Very Short Introduction to *Catholicism*, and not one on *Roman Catholicism*. At the same time, I appreciate the motives of some readers who will mentally add 'Roman' whenever I write of 'the Catholic Church' and 'Catholicism'.

In any case, many elements of Catholic Christianity are found beyond the Catholic Church: for example, the practice of baptism, acceptance of the Four Gospels as normative, and government by bishops. What we may think of as distinctive about Catholicism need not always be uniquely Catholic. Greek, Russian, and other

Orthodox Christians share with Catholics the seven sacraments: baptism, confirmation, the Eucharist, penance or reconciliation after sin, anointing of the sick, ordination, and matrimony. (Sacraments are outward and visible ceremonies, such as using water in baptism, that signify inward, spiritual gifts from God.) This book aims at a wide readership among all those who for various reasons want to learn more about the Catholic Church. I write this book 'from the inside', as one who has been born into a Catholic family and has tried to serve the Catholic and wider community as an ordained priest and teacher of theology. Knowing the institution intimately and identifying with the common faith and deep values of other Catholics, I hope to be able to describe and explain Catholicism competently, but without becoming biased and defensive. Some 'insiders' show an unacceptable bias, but certainly not all. To offer an analogy, when it comes to music or drama, insiders who have years of study, experience, and commitment behind them help us to be more accurately informed about and skilfully guided through musical or dramatic compositions. In such areas, detached outsiders may be able to communicate a wealth of facts, but at times their judgements can remain superficial.

Catholic worship, belief, and practice are not timeless. They have been subject to enormous growth and to changes that embodied either healthy and faithful development or real corruption. How should one construe the ups and downs, the decay and renewal, the happy advances and the tragic disappointments of Catholics through the centuries? The first two chapters of this book will offer an extended tour of that history. Then follow chapters that describe the central beliefs of the Catholic Church about God and the human condition (Chapter 3); the Church and her sacramental life (Chapter 4); and her moral life and teaching (Chapter 5). The book will close by summarizing certain basic characteristics of Catholicism (Chapter 6), and expounding some urgent issues confronting Catholicism and its future (Chapter 7).

In telling the story of Catholicism, every attempt to generalize is constantly beset with enough exceptions to break the rule. But some generalizations will find much support: the coexistence from the beginning of holiness and sinfulness; the recurrent tensions between local communities and a centralized institution; the Catholic Church's challenges to prevailing cultures along with widespread assimilation of them; and shifting relations between governments and the Church.

With deep gratitude I record my warm thanks to those whose questions, criticisms, suggestions, and support have helped me in writing this book: above all, Stephanie Bennett, Vivian Boland, Louis Caruana, Samantha Chant, Dushan Croos, Kerstin Demata, Michael Elligate, Mary Grey, Emmanuel Gurumombe, Michael Hayes, Jane Jeffes, David Jones, Andrea Keagan, Patrick Madigan, Paul Murray, Anthony Nye, Adrian Porter, Glenn Richardson, Trevor Stammers, Anthony Towey, Peter Tyler, Samantha Walcot, and several anonymous advisers for the Oxford University Press.

I dedicate this work to Michael Hayes and other treasured colleagues at St Mary's University College.

Gerald O'Collins, S.J.
St Mary's University College, Twickenham, London
Easter 2008

Abbreviations

Dei Verbum (the Word of God) Vatican II, Dogmatic Constitution on Divine Revelation, 1965

Gaudium et Spes (Joy and Hope) Vatican II, Pastoral Constitution on the Church in the Modern World, 1965

Lumen Gentium (the Light of the Nations) Vatican II, Dogmatic Constitution on the Church, 1964

Nostra Aetate (In Our Age) Vatican II, Declaration on the Relation of the Church to Non-Christian Religions, 1965

Sacrosanctum Concilium (the Sacred Council) Vatican II, Constitution on the Sacred Liturgy, 1963

Unitatis Redintegratio (the Restoration of Unity) Vatican II, Decree on Ecumenism, 1964

List of illustrations

The publisher and the author apologize for any errors or omissions in the above list. If contacted they will be pleased to rectify these at the earliest opportunity.

Chapter 1
From Pentecost to Christopher Columbus (AD 30–1492)

During his life and at his death, Pope John Paul II showed the face of Catholicism to the world. But was there, from the origins of Christianity, a recognizable entity that had some shape and structure and that we might call the nascent Catholic Church? Can we identify, right from the first Pentecost (the Jewish feast when the Holy Spirit descended upon 120 disciples of Jesus (Acts 2: 1–4)), some kind of institution whose history could be written? By answering yes to these questions, this chapter opens the story of Catholic Christianity in Jerusalem after the resurrection of the crucified Jesus (most likely in April AD 30) and the outpouring of the Holy Spirit.

After Pentecost

During his public ministry, Jesus led a revival movement that remained largely within Judaism itself but had some surprising features: above all, his scandalous claim to a personal authority that put him on a par with the God whom he called 'Abba' (Father dear). From a wider group of disciples (who included some non-Jews), he chose a core group of twelve men (all Jews) – a gesture that indicated his intention to re-found the twelve tribes of Israel, or the Jewish nation descended from Abraham and Sarah.

The first Christians expected the risen Christ to return shortly in glory to judge the world. Totally focused on Jesus, they fashioned their interpretation and proclamation of him by putting together two elements: on the one hand, their experience of the events in which he had been the central protagonist and, on the other, the concepts, expectations, and practices that they found to be relevant and illuminating within Judaism. To articulate their convictions about Jesus and his role in fulfilling the divine purposes, they depended in part upon their Jewish heritage. Thus their initiation rite of baptism took over some values from purificatory rites of Judaism, not least from the baptism for the forgiveness of sins practised by John the Baptist. All the followers of Jesus continued to find in the Jewish psalms their main prayerbook. Some or even many of them continued to worship as Jews and in the Jerusalem Temple until excommunicated from Palestinian and other synagogues in the course of the 1st century. At least initially, Jesus' followers were unsure about the need to continue observing the Torah or Jewish law (especially about circumcision and dietary requirements) and the conditions they should impose on Gentiles who accepted faith in the crucified and risen Jesus. Yet the first Christians differed from other devout Jews by administering baptism 'in the name of Jesus' (e.g. Acts 2: 38) and celebrating together the Eucharist, the service in which bread and wine are consecrated and consumed (e.g. Acts 2: 42, 45).

In the Acts of the Apostles, Luke tells the story of the origin and early spread of Christian faith. In the early chapters, Peter functions prominently as the head of the twelve apostles, the core group of public witnesses to Jesus' life, death, and resurrection. With his dramatic calling on the road to Damascus around AD 36, Paul enters the Acts of the Apostles in ch. 9 and takes over the narrative from ch. 15. When Paul returns to Jerusalem in ch. 21, he meets James and 'all the elders'. But there is no mention of Peter still being in Jerusalem. Acts ends with Paul arriving in Rome several years before he and Peter died there as martyrs (between AD 64 and 67). James, a relative of Jesus and the leader of the Mother Church, had already been martyred in Jerusalem.

These first decades of Christian history featured the tension between two 'constituencies', the original Jerusalem Church with its vision of a Torah-observant community and the non-Torah-focused vision of Paul and others. The latter vision lifted the early Church beyond being merely a reform group within Judaism. Paul loved the Jerusalem community and showed that love by collecting money for them from other (local) churches (e.g. 2 Cor. 8: 1–9: 15). Nevertheless, a worldwide identity of Christians in Antioch, Rome, and further centres was formed in a tensional relationship with the Jerusalem community.

Paul spearheaded missionary activity around the Mediterranean world, and spread faith in Jesus as Lord and Saviour. Luke understands this original Christian expansion as opening up an indefinitely long period which will close when Jesus appears again in his glory. In the meantime, as Acts repeatedly indicates, the risen Jesus and his Holy Spirit constantly guide and empower Christian life and mission.

By the 60s, the followers of Jesus had come to be called 'Christians' (Acts 11: 26). Through baptism in the name of Jesus, they knew their sins to be forgiven, received the Holy Spirit, entered the community of the Church, and celebrated the Eucharist. When praying, they called on God as 'Abba' (Rom. 8: 15; Gal. 4: 6), and used not only the psalms but also the Lord's Prayer and other such prayers as the *Benedictus* and the *Magnificat* (Luke 1: 46–55, 68–79), which were originally in Greek like the rest of Luke's Gospel but were subsequently known by their Latin titles. They learned the teaching of Jesus that reached them through their apostolic leaders and their associates. They confessed the risen and exalted Jesus to be Messiah (anointed Deliverer), Lord, and Son of God, and to have sent them, together with God the Father, the gift of the Holy Spirit. They believed that

3

the Spirit was offered to all peoples and that salvation no longer required circumcision and the practice of the Mosaic law in all its details (Acts 15: 1–35).

Paul's letters defend God's gift of salvation to all alike; justification is not gained through human efforts at fulfilling the Jewish law. Faith and baptism incorporate people into the Church, the Body of Christ, and put an end to distinctions between Jew and Gentile, slave and free, male and female (Gal. 3: 26–9). Faith in God the Father, in Jesus as Son of God and divine Lord, and in the Holy Spirit brings all believers together in the unity of baptism, the Eucharist, and a common life. The apostle insists that sharing in the one Eucharistic bread and in the one cup means belonging to the one Body of Christ (1 Cor. 10: 16–17).

While emphasizing the holy unity of the baptized, the apostle's letters let us glimpse the moral failures of early Christians. The First Letter to the Corinthians reveals how some suffered from factionalism, indulged doubts over the central truth of the resurrection, committed fornication, incest, and drunkenness, and showed a selfish unconcern for poorer Christians. The reproaches coming from Paul challenge illusions about a hypothetical golden age of Catholic Christianity that practised heroic ideals on all sides. From the outset, the Church suffered from scandals and divisions. The Book of Revelation, with its opening letters to the seven churches, joins the apostle in testifying to the mixture of holiness and sinfulness that characterized Christianity from the beginning (Rev. 2: 2–3: 22).

Along with holiness and sinfulness, a missionary outreach characterized early Christianity. The Acts of the Apostles and Paul's letters name with respect missionaries who spread the good news about Jesus as Saviour of the world: Barnabas, Epaphroditus, Timothy, Titus, and, not least, Prisca (Priscilla) and Aquila. This married couple, when they lived in Ephesus and Rome, gathered believers in their home, and were also known to the Christians of Corinth (1 Cor. 16: 19; Acts 18: 2–3, 26). Paul calls this couple his 'fellow workers' (Rom. 16: 3). When listing other collaborators on his mission for Christ, he names Andronicus and Junia (another married couple?) as 'distinguished in the eyes of the apostles' (Rom. 16: 7).

Early leadership

In concluding his Letter to the Romans, Paul begins with 'our sister Phoebe, a deacon of the church', writes of those who 'work' to spread the good news, and greets 26 people, 24 of them by name. The final chapter of Romans raises the question: was the Church meant to be a completely egalitarian community, free of any kind of subordination to office-holders and sacred authorities? Did the vision of Jesus and the spontaneous direction of the Holy Spirit exclude such institutionalized leadership as occurred in the subsequent transmission of a threefold ministry of bishops, priests, and deacons? Did that historical development betray Jesus' original dream of male and female disciples as co-partners variously empowered by the Holy Spirit to minister to the whole community? Or was there always some kind of leadership that rightly developed and was handed on to successive generations for the good of all?

We find multiple evidence for the fact that during his ministry Jesus chose twelve disciples from among the wider ranks of his followers and gave them some kind of authoritative office and leadership role. Mark attests the original call and subsequent mission of the Twelve (Mark 3: 13–19; 6: 7–13). Q (*Quelle*, or 'source'), a collection of sayings of Jesus that both Matthew and Luke draw from, implies the existence of his core group (Matt. 19: 28 = Luke 22: 30). They are 'in place' to receive together an appearance of the risen Christ, a fact first attested by a traditional formula cited by Paul (1 Cor. 15: 5) and subsequently narrated in various ways by the Easter chapters of the Gospels. The Twelve are given authority by Christ to lead and teach in his name, a role for which, as Luke and (in his own way) John indicate, they are empowered by the Holy Spirit. Their apostolic mission shares in and comes from the mission of the Son and the Holy Spirit.

What do the Pauline letters indicate about leadership in the Church? A dramatic encounter with the risen Christ made Paul himself an apostle who proclaims the resurrection of the crucified Jesus (1 Cor. 9: 1–2; 15: 8–11; Gal. 1: 11–12, 15–17). Paul's forceful sense of his own apostolic authority comes across clearly, not least in his Letter to the Galatians. After founding communities, he exercises remote authority over them through his letters, messengers, and occasional visits. But how does he understand the authoritative ministry of others in the growing Church?

Paul notes how, within the whole 'Body of Christ', God has appointed various persons to be apostles, prophets, teachers, workers of miracles, healers, helpers, administrators, and speakers in different kinds of tongues (1 Cor. 12: 8–11, 18–30). The apostle's language in 1 Corinthians 12 has encouraged some to envisage a Spirit-filled community with no permanent institutions and ordained officers. But does Paul intend here to issue permanent prescriptions for Church order by setting special, personal gifts of the Spirit ('charisms') above any institutions and offices? It seems rather that he intends to give some practical advice to the Corinthian community and help solve some particular challenges facing their unity in Christ. The eight ministries of 1 Corinthians 12: 28 become five in another list, from a later letter: 'his [Christ's] gifts were that some should be apostles, some prophets, some evangelists, some pastors, and teachers' (Eph. 4: 11). The list now includes 'evangelists' or messengers/preachers of the good news (see Rom. 10: 8–17).

The foundation of many local churches by apostles and others brought a shift in leadership. Settled pastors (called 'overseers', 'elders', and 'deacons') took over from the missionary apostles and other evangelists (see e.g. Acts 20: 17, 28; Phil. 1: 1; 1 Pet. 5: 1–4).

The Pastoral Letters to Timothy and Titus, when recording a more developed organization of ministries, speak of 'overseers' or 'bishops' and their qualifications (1 Tim. 3: 1–7), of the 'elders' or 'presbyters' to be appointed by Titus 'in every town' (Titus 1: 5–6), and of the qualifications appropriate for 'deacons' (1 Tim. 3: 8–10, 12–13), and, apparently, also for 'deaconesses' (1 Tim. 3: 11). Much is stated about the teaching, preaching, defence of sound doctrine, administration, and domestic behaviour expected from leaders in the Church. But apart from some incidental regulations concerning worship (1 Tim. 2: 1–2, 8) and several references to the 'laying on of hands' (e.g. 1 Tim. 5: 22), nothing further is said about the religious ceremonies of the community or about the roles taken by leaders in baptizing, celebrating the Eucharist, and other rites of worship.

An examination of the New Testament supports the conclusion: Christian communities, both at the start (AD 30–70) and then later in the 1st century (AD 70–100), were characterized by a measure of organization. This organization, along with the basic equality of all the baptized, comprised the leaders (with their institutionalized offices) and the led (with their personal gifts). These communities were not simply and totally egalitarian.

We find in St Ignatius of Antioch (d. around AD 107) a key witness to the emerging structure of Catholic Christianity. The first writer known to have used the expression 'the Catholic Church' (*Epistle to the Smyrnaeans*, 8. 2), this martyr upheld worldwide, 'catholic' unity of belief and conduct. On the local scene, 'Catholicism' meant obedience to a monarchical or single presiding bishop, supported by presbyters and deacons. The bishop was to preside at the celebration of the Eucharist, defend the centrality of Christ's bodily resurrection, and approve the marriage of Christians.

Irenaeus of Lyons (d. around AD 200) stressed continuity in the orthodox teaching of bishops, who succeeded one another when the ministry of the apostles gave way to a continuous line of ordained bishops. In the worldwide Church, their succession could be traced back to the apostles – something Irenaeus did for the sees of Ephesus, Smyrna, and Rome, 'the greatest and oldest church' (*Adversus Haereses*, 3. 1–4). This championing of bishops as faithful teachers in the Church also entailed recognizing the authority of the apostolic scriptures and rejecting the new 'scriptures', produced by Gnostic movements that emerged after AD 150 on the margins of Christianity. Gnosticism drew on Jewish, Christian, and pagan sources to present salvation as involving not a resurrection of the body but the immortal, human spirit escaping from an evil, material world and returning to the heavenly world from which it had come.

Martyrdom

Persecution and martyrdom, inflicted particularly on Christian leaders, began very early. In AD 44 James the son of Zebedee was beheaded by the order of Herod Agrippa I. Paul lists the imprisonments, floggings, and other sufferings he had already undergone by the late 50s (2 Cor. 11: 23–7). Before his Damascus Road encounter with the risen Christ, he himself had acquiesced in the stoning of Stephen (Acts 7: 55–8: 1). In AD 62, the Jerusalem community lost its leader when James, a relative of Jesus, was stoned to death. Various records of martyrdoms have survived. In his *Annals* (15. 44), the Roman historian Tacitus tells the gruesome story of Christians killed as scapegoats by Emperor Nero in AD 64:

> Covered with the skins of beasts, they were torn by dogs and perished; or were nailed to crosses; or were doomed to the flames and burnt, to provide illumination at night when there was no more daylight.

The *Passion of St Perpetua* describes how she and other Christians in Carthage were mauled by wild beasts and then had their throats cut in AD 203, during a persecution under Emperor Septimius Severus.

When Church leaders met for the First Council of Nicaea in AD 325, not a few of them showed the marks of persecution on their bodies. The hands of Paul of Neocaesarea had been paralysed by hot irons. Hosius, the bishop of Cordoba who acted as Emperor Constantine's adviser at the Council, and Eustathius, bishop of Antioch 324–30, had both suffered during the cruel persecution of Maximin Daza (d. 313). Two Egyptian bishops had each lost an eye. One of them, Paphnutius, had also been hamstrung. His scarred body evoked the veneration of the bishops and others present. Emperor Constantine showed respect by kissing his mutilated face.

Growth of Christianity

During the period of the Roman persecution, many pagans owed their lives to their Christian neighbours. By courageously caring for the sick, Christians saved numerous people during the epidemics of AD 165–80 and 251–66, which destroyed almost one-third of the population of the Roman world. These calamitous crises became the occasion for converting to the Church and being baptized.

Baptism 'in the name of the Father and of the Son and of the Holy Spirit', reported at the very end of Matthew's Gospel, rapidly became and remained the standard formula for the basic sacrament or rite of Christian initiation. The *Didache*, written probably around AD 90 and so one of the earliest Christian works outside the New Testament, instructs those who baptize to do so by using the Trinitarian formula (7. 1–3). The invocation of the Trinity provided the creative ground-plan for constructing the questions ('Do you believe in God the Father?' and so forth) and the answers that led to the formation of creeds, or brief summaries of Christian belief. With the Old Roman Creed crystallizing around the middle of the 3rd century, baptismal creeds developed in the West and the East and would be followed by the creed from the First Council of Nicaea (325).

The celebration of the Eucharist on Sunday, or the Lord's Day, reaches back to the start of Christianity. Since it was on that day that they first came to know of Jesus' resurrection from the dead, the earliest (Jewish) disciples took the momentous step of moving their day of worship from the Jewish Sabbath to the Christian Sunday. Eucharistic worship comprised two parts: the Liturgy of the Word, which followed the pattern of Jewish synagogue services and consisted of prayers, hymns, and readings from the Bible; and the Liturgy of the Eucharist, which drew on Jesus' words at the Last Supper, included an invocation of the Holy Spirit (the *epiclesis*), and involved consecrating bread and wine into the body and blood of Christ.

The relationship with Judaism

Popular thinking often takes the tragic destruction of Jerusalem in AD 70 to mark a definitive parting of the ways between the Church and Judaism. Yet in the 2nd century, Justin Martyr (who came from the Holy Land and died in Rome around AD 165) in his *Dialogue with Trypho* shared the Hebrew scriptures with the Jew Trypho and never belittled the faith of his debating partner.

A younger contemporary of Justin, Irenaeus of Lyons, set his face against the anti-Jewish aberrations of Marcion, who rejected the Creator God of the Old Testament as a cruel deity, not to be identified with the Father of our Lord Jesus Christ. Coming from Asia Minor and resident for a time in Rome, Marcion excluded all the Jewish scriptures and accepted only an emended version of Luke's Gospel and ten Pauline letters. Thus he wanted to strip Christianity both of its Jewish roots and of those Christian scriptures (in particular, Matthew's Gospel) that were particularly concerned to justify Christian faith as fulfilling the Old Testament history and scriptures. Against such errors, Irenaeus championed not merely the four Gospels but also the enduring value of the Jewish scriptures and, in particular, their doctrine of God. There is only one God, who created the material world and made human beings in the divine image and likeness (Gen. 1: 27).

In the late 4th century, a section of *The Incarnation of the Word* (7. 33–40) by Athanasius shows how contact and debate with Jews still mattered to a bishop of Alexandria. And as a hermit in the Syrian desert, Jerome (d. AD 420) learned Hebrew from a Jewish scholar, enabling him to produce what came to be called the Vulgate, the most widely used Latin translation of the Bible; he translated the Hebrew scriptures directly from the original texts. But, sadly, by the end of the 4th century, this spirit of cooperation had changed: the misinterpretation of the cry of the crowd at the Jesus' condemnation in Matthew 27: 25 ('his blood be on us and on our children'), the polemic against 'the Jews' in John's Gospel, some severe language from Paul (e.g. 1 Thess. 2: 14–16), and other texts and factors had encouraged anti-Jewish attitudes among Christians. With John Chrysostom (d. AD 407), archbishop of Constantinople, anti-Jewish polemics firmly set in. Through many centuries Catholics committed terrible crimes against Jews or remained guilty bystanders of such crimes. It would only be with Pope John XXIII (d. 1963), the Second Vatican Council (1962–5), and Pope John Paul II (d. 2005) that a decisively clear change of direction came in teaching and practice. The Second Vatican Council called for repentance and denounced 'the hatred, persecutions, and displays of anti-Semitism directed against Jews at any time and from any source' (*Nostra Aetate*, 4).

Constantine and controversies

Constantine's decisive victory of 28 October 312 on the outskirts of Rome made him the Emperor of the Western Empire. Before engaging the forces of Maxentius, his rival for power, Constantine reputedly had a vision of Christ's cross and the words: 'in this sign you will conquer'. With the sign of the cross on his own helmet and his soldiers' shields, he believed that the one, all-powerful God guaranteed the military triumph. The 313 Edict of Milan, a verbal agreement reached between Constantine and Licinius, the Emperor of the Eastern Empire, pledged religious freedom for Christians and the restitution of goods confiscated from them during the severe persecution decreed by Emperor Diocletian in February 303 and continuing until 310.

Christians experienced a startling reversal of fortune when Constantine initiated a long series of legislative acts in their favour. In March 321, he decreed Sunday to be a day of rest. In 324, public money became available for the construction of churches, and in 326 Constantine, encouraged by his elderly mother, Helena (d. around 330), began building the central shrine of Christendom, the Church of the Resurrection in Jerusalem. He had already started building St Peter's Basilica in Rome, sited on the place of the apostle's martyrdom and burial, and completed in 328.

Visitors to St Peter's (reconstructed in the 16th and 17th centuries according to plans drawn up by Bramante, Raphael, Michelangelo, and other artistic geniuses) can stop in the portico to gaze at the statues of two emperors, each astride a horse: Constantine and Charlemagne (who was crowned in St Peter's on Christmas Day 800 as the first emperor of the Holy Roman Empire). Were they saviours or masters of the Church? However we judge their impact on Christian life, Constantine, by tolerating and then encouraging Christianity, brought no separation of Church and state. It was he who convened, funded, and (at least initially) presided at the first General Council, that of Nicaea in 325. He legislated for orthodox faith, outlawed heresy, and (even though he was not baptized until shortly before his death in 337) preached weekly sermons to his courtiers. Henceforth Christianity and, in particular, Catholic Christians would continue to struggle with

Church–state relations – under monarchies, dictatorships, oligarchies, democracies, and all manner of variants in these systems of government.

Toleration had hardly arrived under Constantine before Christians found themselves embroiled in the first of three major struggles for their faith in Christ.

First, Arius, a priest from Egypt, began communicating through his preaching and popular songs the notion that the Son of God was only a created being and hence did not share in the eternal existence of the Father. The bishops at the First Council of Nicaea (325), also called Nicaea I, spoke out clearly for the divine identity of the Son and declared him to be 'true God from true God, begotten, not made, of one being/substance with the Father'. The Council left indelibly printed on the conscience of Catholics (and other Christians) a deep faith in the divinity of Christ. This faith remained for them a non-negotiable truth.

Then, within 50 years, Apollinarius, a bishop of Laodicaea (in Asia Minor), began defending a position at the other extreme from Arius. Utterly intent on defending the Nicene faith in Christ's divinity, Apollinarius maintained that in the incarnation the Logos, or Word of God, assumed a living body but took the place in Christ of the higher (rational) soul. Hence Apollinarius did not accept a complete humanity in Christ: he was truly divine but, by lacking a rational soul, he was not fully human. By condemning Apollinarius, the First Council of Constantinople (381), also called Constantinople I, upheld the complete humanity that the Word of God had assumed.

Granted, then, that Christ was and is truly divine (Nicaea I) and fully human (Constantinople I), how is the *union* between his divinity and humanity to be understood and interpreted? The Council of Ephesus (431) taught that his divinity and humanity are not *separated*; as if Christ were divided up into two agents: the

Word of God and the man Jesus. Twenty years later, the Council of Chalcedon (451) added that the divinity and humanity of Christ (his two 'natures') are not merged together but remain truly *distinct*. The one person of Christ existed and exists in two complete (distinct but not separate) natures, with all the attributes that belong essentially to those two natures.

The break between East and West

Across the Bosphorus from Constantinople, Chalcedon was at the heart of the Eastern (Roman) Empire. But an essential contribution to the Council's teaching came from the West, through a letter from Pope Leo I, who would be known as 'Leo the Great'. At Chalcedon, more than 500 bishops approved this letter from 'the most blessed and most holy Archbishop Leo … since it agrees with the confession of the great [St] Peter and is a pillar of support to all against the heterodox'. A year later, it was Leo the Great, and not a Roman emperor, who persuaded Attila, king of the Huns and known as 'the Scourge of God', not to sack Rome. In the next century, Gregory the Great (pope 590–604) did much to re-found Catholic Christianity in Britain by sending St Augustine to England, where he landed in Kent during the summer of 597. There were difficulties between this somewhat timid monk and representatives of the ancient Celtic Church. But the success of Augustine's mission was sealed when he was consecrated the first archbishop of Canterbury. An English Christianity emerged that happily mingled Anglo-Saxon, Celtic, and Roman elements.

Five months after his election to the papacy, Gregory the Great in a circular letter of February 591 to five Eastern patriarchs declared that he venerated the first four Councils (Nicaea I, Constantinople I, Ephesus, and Chalcedon), just as he venerated the four Gospels. Even late in the day, his endorsement of Constantinople I (381) and the Creed it developed on the basis of Nicaea I, definitively clarified the status of that second Council for the universal Church and showed a proper sensitivity to East–West relations. Since none of its bishops had taken part in Constantinople I, the Western Church had been slow to recognize the authority of that council and its Creed.

By the late 9th century, Eastern theologians began accusing Western Catholics of unilaterally tampering with the Nicene-Constantinopolitan Creed by adding the 'Filioque', or teaching about the Holy Spirit 'proceeding' not only from the Father but also from the Son. Charlemagne (d. 814) accepted these fateful words (that had been added earlier, probably at the Fourth Synod of Braga (675)) when he encouraged the chanting of the Creed at Mass throughout his empire. The addition was eventually adapted in Rome when Emperor Henry II in 1013 ordered the Latin Church everywhere to insert the 'Filioque' when they sang or recited the Creed.

For a century or more, few outstanding popes had been elected. Sergius III (pope 904–11) was said to have murdered his two predecessors, and John XII (pope 955–64) was given the papal office at the age of 20 through the influence of his powerful father. Between 882 and 984, nine popes were murdered by poison, strangulation, and other methods. That was the darkest hour of the papacy, which appalled even the dissolute world of 10th-century Rome. This deplorable period also helped trigger a lasting schism between Western Catholicism and Orthodox (Greek for 'right belief') Christianity, a break conventionally dated to a day in 1054 when the patriarch of Constantinople and the leader of a delegation from Rome mutually excommunicated one another.

The schism between East and West was, however, never complete; some, albeit only a minority, of Eastern-rite Christians have remained in communion with the Bishop of Rome. Yet the split affected the governance of the Catholic Church. It helped to encourage a Western, over-centralized system focused on the pope rather than normal governance through regional synods or

2. Pope Paul VI and Athenagoras, the Ecumenical Patriarch of Constantinople and head of Orthodox Christians, embrace on the Pope's arrival in Istanbul, 25 July 1967

assemblies of bishops – the system that characterizes Eastern Christianity.

Bishops, monks, and missionaries

Catholic and other Christians have never stopped finding inspiration from many bishops, monks, and missionaries who led and spread the Church in the first millennium and beyond. St Augustine (354–430), bishop of Hippo in North Africa, was the first and, arguably, the greatest of an 'A' team of three theologians who moulded Western Catholic thought for all time. The other two on this team are St Anselm (d. 1109 as archbishop of Canterbury) and the priest and Dominican professor, St Thomas Aquinas (d. 1274).

Monasticism may be described as a movement among baptized Christians who respond to Christ's call to perfection by giving themselves, through poverty, celibacy, and obedience, to a life of prayer, worship in common, and the service of others. In the 4th century, St Basil of Caesarea (d. 379) and his sister St Macrina the Younger (d. around 380) contributed to the rise of Eastern monasticism. That in turn helped the rise of Western monasticism. St Benedict of Nursia (d. around 550), after living as a hermit in a cave at Subiaco (outside Rome), gathered followers and founded twelve monastic communities, each with twelve monks and an abbot appointed by Benedict. His sister, St Scholastica (d. around 543), who founded a convent a few miles from Monte Cassino, is buried in the same grave as her brother. Their monastic way of life proved a haven in an unsettled society, and helped to preserve some of the literature and art forms from the Graeco-Roman culture.

Despite incessant invasions of Germanic and other Northern tribes, sacred and secular learning remained alive, thanks to such leaders as St Hilda of Whitby (d. 680), St Bede 'the Venerable' (d. 735), and many other men and women who followed the monastic way of life. Dated from around 800, the glorious writing and illustrations of the Book of Kells (from a monastery in County Meath but preserved in Trinity College, Dublin) set forth the four Gospels. That manuscript glows like a jewel in bearing witness to the monastic love for the scriptures, in general, and for the life of Christ, in particular.

Apparently born in Roman Britain, St Patrick (d. around 461) spent six years as a slave in Ireland before escaping back to Britain. After training for Christian ministry, he returned to Ireland as a bishop, made Armagh his episcopal see, and set himself to evangelize the whole island. The daughter of one couple he baptized, St Brigid (d. around 523), founded at Kildare the first nunnery in Ireland and exercised much influence in the growth of Catholic Christianity. After Patrick, she was to become the second patron saint of Ireland.

In the 6th century, large monastic communities began to grow in Ireland, and for many centuries ecclesiastical authority was exercised by the abbots (and abbesses) of these monasteries. Some abbots, like St Columba (d. 597) and St Columbanus (d. 615), left Ireland and became missionaries abroad: the former in Scotland and the latter in Gaul, Switzerland, and northern Italy. These Celtic monk-missionaries, along with their Anglo-Saxon counterparts, established new monasteries – such as Columba's foundation on the Island of Iona, off the Scottish coast – and spread the practice of 'private' penance or 'auricular' (in the ear) confession of sins. Eventually such private confession of sins became standard and replaced the original system of public penance.

Cathedrals, religious orders, and pilgrimages

Any account of Catholicism from the 11th to the end of the 15th century will concentrate on Europe, as that is where the overwhelming majority of Catholics then lived. But the discovery of the Americas in 1492 by Christopher Columbus (1451–1506) and other subsequent events would make the situation dramatically different at the end of the 20th century. By the year 2000, three-quarters of the world's one billion Catholics were living in the Americas (North, Central, and South), Africa, Asia, and Oceania.

Church buildings from the 11th to the beginning of the 16th century bear eloquent witness to the Catholicism of those centuries, when all classes of society collaborated to express their faith through mosaics, carvings, paintings, stained-glass windows, and the churches and monasteries that housed them. From around AD 1000 until the 13th century, Romanesque style (and its variant in Norman style) dominated – with massive walls, relatively small windows, and round arches and vaults. The Romanesque basilica of Vézelay (south-east of Paris), Durham cathedral, and the Norman (with Arab decoration) abbey of

3. Famous for its stained-glass windows and exterior sculptures, Chartres embodies Gothic cathedrals at their best and humanity rising towards God

Monreale, near Palermo, offer outstanding examples from those centuries. The 12th-century mosaics of Monreale represent an entire cycle of Old Testament and New Testament stories and figures, with a gigantic Christ conferring his blessing and enthroned in the central apse.

Gothic style began with the rebuilding of the royal abbey church of Saint-Denis (near Paris), which was dedicated in 1144. Pointed arches, soaring towers, and the light that streamed through the walls of brilliant stained glass lifted human minds and hearts to God. The Gothic cathedrals of Chartres (begun 1145) and Amiens (begun 1220) became models for churches right across Europe. The rich sculpture, stained glass, and luminous structure of Chartres Cathedral (south-west of Paris) have always inspired superlatives. Through stone, wood, and glass, medieval Catholics set down for all time the story of their faith.

Along with the visible heritage of Catholicism, one should not forget the musical life that flourished in Eastern and Western worship. The worship of Eastern Christians, whether Orthodox or Catholic, is enriched by liturgical hymns, some as old as the 5th and 6th centuries. The medieval repertoire of plainchant and the glory of polyphony belong among the treasures of Western civilization, and have enjoyed an extraordinary revival in many parts of the world.

From the time of the Emperor Charlemagne, Benedictine abbeys had spread across Europe, but by medieval times some of them had lost their original fervour. A reform movement led to the foundation of new communities where stricter observance prevailed. Thus the Cistercian Order emerged, its name coming from its mother house in Cîteaux, where St Bernard (1090–1153) became a novice in 1112. His immense influence played a major part in disseminating the new order right across Western Europe. By the close of the 12th century, 530 Cistercian abbeys had been established, and there would be a further 150 foundations in the next century. Bernard sent a group of monks to found the Abbey of Rievaulx in Yorkshire. By the time of St Aelred (abbot 1147–67, and called the 'Bernard of the North'), this community numbered around 600 monks. Like Rievaulx, Cistercian houses were normally erected in remote areas. They followed strict rules on silence, diet, and manual labour, fostered plain architecture, and practised efficient and enterprising farming methods.

Along with reactions to decadence, a new, tender devotion to Jesus in his humanity worked to encourage fresh initiatives in religious life. Where the Cistercians represented a 'flight from the world', the 'mendicant' ('living by begging') orders of Dominicans and Franciscans also revitalized medieval Catholicism but in different ways.

St Dominic (d. 1221), the founder of the Order of Preachers (commonly called the Dominicans), worked untiringly to spread true Christian doctrine. A courageous and efficient leader, he parted ways with the careerism of many upwardly mobile priests by three times refusing to accept nomination as a bishop. Dominican preachers popularized the practice of the rosary, still a very common devotion among Catholics and some other Christians. It commemorates events involving Christ or his mother Mary and requires a string of beads to count the particular prayers it involves. The five 'joyful mysteries' centre on Christ's birth and childhood. The (recently added) five 'mysteries of light' begin with Christ's baptism and end with his institution of the Eucharist. The five 'sorrowful mysteries' open with Christ's agony in the garden and end with his death on the cross. The five 'glorious mysteries' start with Christ's resurrection and close with Mary's sharing in her Son's victory over death. Each mystery includes the 'Our Father' (once), the 'Hail Mary' (ten times), and the 'Glory be to the Father' (once).

The Dominicans propagated the rosary; the Franciscans did the same for the Christmas crib and the Stations of the Cross (a devotion in which the participants pray as they move around fourteen scenes from the suffering and death of Christ). These devotions flowed straight out of the very Jesus-centred life of St Francis of Assisi (d. 1226). By celebrating Christmas in a barn with animals and straw, Francis conveyed the deep meaning of Jesus' birth and initiated the practice of using various figures to represent it through what we know as Christmas cribs or crèches. During an ecstatic experience two years before his death, Francis received the stigmata – wounds on his hands, feet, and side that corresponded to those of the crucified Jesus and so completed the Christ-like image he presented. The followers of Francis took over in 1342 the custody of the shrines in Jerusalem associated with Christ's suffering and death. For those Christians unable to visit the Holy Land, Franciscans led the way in erecting innumerable Stations of the Cross as a means for sharing through prayer in the passion, death, and burial of Jesus.

The influence of Francis and his associate, St Clare (1194–1253), has endured through such figures as St Antony of Padua

4. Young people holding high the cross on their annual pilgrimage to the shrine of Maipu, Chile

(1195–1231), Blessed Angela of Foligno (d. 1309), St Pio of Pietralcina (1887–1968), and other Franciscan mystics and missionaries. The humility, total poverty, and Christ-like love practised by Francis have made him one of the most popular saints of all time.

At the age of 35, Dante Alighieri (1265–1321) joined other pilgrims by coming to Rome for the 'Jubilee Year' of 1300, the first of 25 Jubilee Years that have brought Catholics to Rome down to 2000. These Jubilee Years offer particular spiritual benefits to those who come on pilgrimage to Rome and perform various religious exercises. Pilgrimages stretch back to the origins of the whole Jewish-Christian story. Abraham and Sarah left Ur of the Chaldees and became nomads for God. New Testament books such as the Letter to the Hebrews and the First Letter of Peter saw human life as a journey to the heavenly homeland. By AD 250, the cult of Peter and Paul began to flourish in Rome and drew pilgrims to their tombs. A work from the end of the 4th century, the *Pilgrimage of Etheria*, told the story of a pilgrim (probably a Spaniard) who visited Jerusalem and its neighbourhood. She described in detail the liturgical ceremonies: not only the daily and Sunday offices but also the services for the Epiphany, Holy Week (including the procession of palms to the Mount of Olives, and the veneration of the cross), Easter, and Pentecost. Dante used the pilgrimage theme to open the *Comedy* ('In the middle of our life's road I found myself in a dark wood – the straight way ahead lost'); the spiritual transformation of the pilgrim takes him through hell and purgatory to heaven. Along with Jerusalem and Santiago de Compostela (with its tomb of St James the Apostle), both before and after 1300 Rome attracted pilgrims, especially during Jubilee Years.

Not as exalted a poet as Dante, Geoffrey Chaucer (1340–1400) pictured in *The Canterbury Tales* a group of 29 pilgrims on their way to the shrine of St Thomas Becket (d. 1170) in Canterbury Cathedral. This assorted group of men and women allowed

Chaucer to describe the saints and sinners who made up the Catholic Church of his day. Those shared journeys to the shrines of saints embodied a common faith. The ancient Celts named such shrines 'thin places'; time and again, they experienced there close communication with God. Pilgrimages reinforced the consciousness of life as a spiritual journey, a preparation for death and eternal life. In later centuries, pilgrimages have also played a role in maintaining a sense of national identity. Thus, for example, devotion to the Blessed Virgin Mary at her shrine of Czestochowa continues to shape Catholicism in Poland.

The Crusades

After the scandalous low of the 10th-century papacy, the second thousand years of Catholicism began with Sylvester II (pope 999–1003), a pope committed to promoting the healthy state of the Church. A longer papacy allowed Gregory VII (pope 1073–85) to work more vigorously towards reforming money-hungry and sexually immoral clergy and opposing secular rulers who meddled in the election of bishops and similar matters. The Gregorian reforms, while being on balance praiseworthy, suffered from their ambiguities, both within the Catholic Church and beyond. Within the Church, Gregory effected a certain shift of power from the local churches to the Roman See. Corrupt or inept officials of the popes could misuse this new centralism at the expense of the bishops in charge of dioceses.

Relations with 'others' featured in a remarkable letter of 1076 to Anzir, the Muslim king of Mauretania, whom Gregory thanked for freeing some prisoners and promising to free some more. Anzir had even sent a candidate to be consecrated a bishop and so take care of his Christian subjects. Nearly 900 years later, in its Declaration on the Relation of the Church to Non-Christian Religions, the Second Vatican Council recalled this letter, which had recognized how Christians and Muslims honour Abraham and adore the same God. Yet two years earlier, in 1074, Gregory had unsuccessfully planned a military campaign against the Turks.

After the death of Muhammad in Medina (Arabia) in 632, the Arab conquests of Palestine, Syria, Egypt, and North Africa moved ahead fast. Christianity lost vast tracts to Islam. In the 8th century, Muslim forces conquered Spain and were stopped from overrunning the kingdom of the Franks by the victory won in 732 near Poitiers by the soldiers of Charles Martel, the grandfather of Charlemagne. Armed conflicts, as well as a measure of religious and cultural dialogue, were to characterize Christian–Muslim relations in the centuries to come. The Muslim rulers of Spain normally tolerated Christians and Jews, especially in such cultural centres as Cordoba. An outstanding Arab philosopher and polymath, Averroes (1126–98), was born and lived there, and his commentaries on Aristotle exercised a considerable influence on Christian thinkers in Paris and elsewhere. The Jewish philosopher Moses Maimonides (1135–1204) was also born in Cordoba and eventually settled in Old Cairo. Writing in both Hebrew and Arabic, he affected such Christians as Thomas Aquinas by his principal treatise, the *Guide for the Perplexed*, which aimed to synthesize divine revelation with the findings of human reason developed by Aristotle. But the Crusades and the gradual re-conquest of Spain by Christian princes harmed relations with Muslims and Jews.

In a speech delivered at Clermont (France) in 1095, Urban II (pope 1088–99), who had been made a cardinal by Gregory VII and continued his programme of reform, called for a Christian war to recapture the Holy Land from the Muslims. Within a few months the First Crusade was under way. When the Crusaders captured Jerusalem in 1099, they killed around 10,000 Muslims, as well as many Jews. This barbaric slaughter sent shock waves around the Mediterranean world. Christian minorities in Muslim countries experienced hardships they had not known before. In 1204, when the Fourth Crusade switched to Constantinople from its original objective (Egypt), the Crusaders sacked the city and set up the Latin Empire and patriarchate. They achieved only a temporary reunion between the Eastern and Western Churches. The long-term effect of the Fourth Crusade was to seal more or less the schism between Rome and Constantinople and weaken the Eastern Empire against Muslim inroads.

A few years later, in 1236, Christian forces re-conquered Cordoba. When Granada, the last Spanish territory held by the Muslims, surrendered in 1492, the new Christian Spain of Ferdinand and Isabella failed to incorporate its Muslim minority, as well as expelling its Jewish population. A few years earlier (1478), Ferdinand and Isabella had set up the Spanish Inquisition to detect and prosecute heretical views and (sometimes) immoral behaviour. In certain cities during its early days, the Inquisition convicted over 40% of those accused and handed them over to be burnt by the civil authorities. From around the middle of the 16th century, the percentage of trials resulting in capital punishment had dropped to about 1%. The use of torture, the anonymity of witnesses, and other features made the Inquisition enduringly notorious as an efficient instrument of religious and civil control. Among its few redeeming features was the way that, unlike countries in Northern Europe, it hardly ever concerned itself with witchcraft, since its officials normally did not believe that any such thing existed.

Not long before the reign of Ferdinand and Isabella began, the Ottoman Empire, founded around 1300 in Turkey, had captured (Christian) Constantinople in 1453. By the end of the 16th century, the Ottoman power extended from Hungary, through the Balkans and Greece, to Egypt. This new Muslim expansion into Europe was dealt a crushing blow, at least by sea, through the naval forces of the Christian League at the battle of Lepanto (near the Gulf of Corinth) in 1571. On the anniversary of the naval battle at

Lepanto, Pope Pius V instituted the feast of Our Lady of the Rosary to be celebrated on 7 October. Catholics believed themselves to be victorious through the help of the Holy Mother of God, invoked by praying the rosary. The feast confirmed a trend among Spanish and other Catholics to define themselves, in part, by opposition to Muslims. There is no other such religious feast by which Catholics have ever defined themselves against Hindus, Buddhists, or the followers of other world religions.

By the time of the battle of Lepanto, however, the expeditions of Christopher Columbus and the Protestant Reformation had changed forever the direction of Catholic and world history. We turn now to those changes.

Chapter 2
From Christopher Columbus to date (1492–2008)

What has being Catholic meant in different times and at different places over the last 500 years? To organize the themes, we will look in turn at the expansion of Europe, the Reformation, the new learning, and the coming of the world church.

The expansion of Europe

The discoveries initiated by Columbus revealed the existence of millions of human beings in societies that had gone on for many centuries without the slightest chance of hearing about Jesus Christ and joining the Church. The arrival of the Europeans in the Americas raised the issue of universal participation in the benefits of Christ's redemption. How could he have been the Saviour for the indigenous peoples of the Americas? How could they have shared in his redemptive grace without even hearing his name?

In 1271–5, the Venetian Marco Polo visited China and provided the earliest European description of the Far East. This tale of the wealth of 'Cathay' fascinated later generations, including a Genovese sea captain, Christopher Columbus. He thought he could reach Asia when he sailed westward in 1492.

The start of the Western Age of Discovery pre-dates, however, Columbus's crossing of the Atlantic. The Portuguese Prince Henry

the Navigator (1394–1460) promoted the exploration and colonization of the Canaries and the Azores. Under his patronage Portuguese seamen sailed well down the west coast of Africa. In 1487, Bartolomeo Dias (d. 1500) became the first (known) European captain to round the Cape of Good Hope and so open up new sea routes to India and beyond. Within a few years of these Portuguese voyages and Columbus's discovery, Europeans began to circumnavigate the world, to map it, and to name it with European names ('Africa', 'America', 'Asia', and 'Australia'). Western and Christian domination were on the way.

Alexander VI (pope 1492–1503) divided the New World between Spain and Portugal, giving their kings sovereign power over the lands that their subjects were discovering and making them responsible for evangelizing the people of those lands. The Portuguese rulers developed an empire in Africa, America, and the Far East, and sent Catholic missionaries around the world. Apart from Angola, Mozambique, and such small enclaves as East Timor and Goa, the major lasting result of the Portuguese evangelization and colonization remains Brazil, currently the largest Catholic nation in the world; its population of over 190 million people (by 2007) is still predominantly Catholic.

Under Emperor King Charles V, king of Spain from 1516 to 1556, the Spanish Empire spread through Central and South America. In 1521, Mexico fell to Hernándo Cortés; in 1530, Peru was conquered by Francisco Pizarro. Along with or shortly after the violent invasions and massacres committed by the *conquistadores*, Dominicans, Franciscans, and other missionaries arrived and preached the Christian message, sometimes by methods that failed to respect the freedom and religious sensitivities of the Aztecs of Mexico, the Incas of Peru, the Mayas of Yucatán, and other American Indians. Catholicism was established everywhere in Central and South America. Some groups, notably the Mexicans, embraced the new faith as a liberation from certain horrifying customs. The religion of the Aztecs had included human sacrifice, and many such sacrifices were rounded off by cannibalism, with members of the nobility eating the victims.

But the Indian societies were ravaged by invaders in search of gold and devastated by small-pox, other diseases, and alcoholism. The Indian population of Spanish-ruled America declined by at least 75% in the first hundred years of that rule. The collapse of the local population led the *conquistadores* to begin importing black slaves from Africa. Some religious leaders, such as Bartolomé de Las Casas (1474–1566), denounced the crimes committed in the name of Spain and Christianity. Significantly, this courageous Dominican served as bishop of Chiapas (1542–50), a poor diocese in southern Mexico where in the 1990s the Indian population hit world headlines over their struggle for civil and religious rights.

By 1620, 36 bishoprics and countless parishes in Central and South America served the Spanish settlers, Indian converts, and other groups, with everything under the control of two viceroys: one in Peru and the other in New Spain (Mexico). Through the viceroys the running of the colonial state and the organization of the Church depended upon Madrid. Popes had no control, for example, over the appointment of bishops.

One group that maintained its freedom from royal control was the Society of Jesus, which insisted on its primary obedience being to a superior general resident in Rome and through him to the pope. Besides developing colleges and churches in the towns, the Jesuits spread out among the Indian population where their frontier missionary work put into practice the entirely peaceful methods of evangelization advocated by Las Casas. They sometimes succeeded in a remarkable way – as with the Guarani Indians of Paraguay. From 1603, they began settlements, which combined agricultural work, various crafts, and a style of worship that included much music. With the help of coadjutor brothers (non-ordained Jesuits), some of them ex-soldiers who had survived wars in Europe, the missionaries trained the Guaranis to defend themselves effectively against slave traders. The 1767 expulsion of Jesuits from Spanish America brought this missionary work to an end – as dramatically expressed in the film *The Mission* (1986). The ten settlements of the Chiquitos mission, in what became Bolivia, survived the loss of their spiritual leaders somewhat better. There the Jesuit mix of education, agriculture, and religious celebrations integrated even more skilfully the Indian language and culture with Christianity.

A few Jesuits, such as St Peter Claver (1580–1654), spent their lives courageously serving a very different group, the African slaves imported in ever-increasing numbers into Brazil, Cuba, Venezuela, and other lands of the Portuguese and Spanish empires. The slaves provided labour for the sugar plantations and other projects. But Claver enjoyed very little back-up. Many Jesuits and others ministered to the Indians, but the population of black slaves, often much worse treated, were totally subjected to their white owners. The black population came to accept Christianity but sometimes with a West African mix, as in the Afro-Brazilian cults. Catholic Brazil became the last country in the world to abolish slavery officially – only in 1888.

Out in Asia, missionaries such as St Francis Xavier (1506–52) reached India, Sri Lanka, Malacca, the Moluccas, and Japan. One of the first Europeans ever to visit Japan, he created Catholic communities there. Tragically, fear of foreign invasions triggered savage persecutions from the end of the 16th century. Thousands of Catholics suffered death for their faith; in 1640, Japan was closed to all foreigners and Christianity itself totally proscribed. When these restrictions were lifted in the second half of the 19th century, foreign missionaries discovered many hidden Catholics who had secretly kept and handed on their faith. Xavier himself had died on an island south of Canton, while waiting to enter China.

Within a few years of his death, however, other Jesuits entered China. Through his learning in astronomy, languages, and mathematics, the Italian Matteo Ricci (1552–1610) won the freedom to preach the Christian message. The German Jesuit Adam Schall (1591–1666) helped reform the Chinese calendar. By this and other achievements in astronomy (such as the prediction of an eclipse in 1629), the way was open for a Flemish Jesuit, Ferdinand Verbiest (1623–88), to be nominated president of the Chinese Imperial Board of Astronomy. This appointment by the Chinese ruling dynasty signalled the high point of a missionary endeavour that not only combined faith with human learning but also adapted Christian ceremonies to the local culture. This approach accommodated traditional Chinese rituals and beliefs, including the practice of venerating ancestors. The success of this accommodation gave rise to violent controversy

5. Pope John XXIII is carried through St Peter's Square at the opening of the Second Vatican Council (1962–5), the most significant event in 20th-century Catholic history

over the 'Chinese rites'. In 1704, after a century of debate, Clement XI (pope 1700–21) was persuaded to condemn such adaptations as tainted by superstition. The Chinese emperors were outraged; during the 1720s, missionaries and then Christianity itself were banned in China. Eventually, 20th-century popes and the Second Vatican Council (1962–5) were to accept and even encourage adaptation to various cultures and a full role for the local clergy.

This full role came slowly in many places, notably in the Philippines. Evangelization by Dominican, Franciscan, and other missionaries followed the start of Spanish rule in 1565. Even though the majority of Filipinos had been baptized by the end of the 18th century, the indigenous clergy remained in inferior positions. It was only in 1905 that the first Filipino bishop was appointed. Pope Pius XI, however, encouraged local leadership. In 1926, he personally consecrated six Chinese bishops; in 1936, he appointed the first Japanese archbishop of Tokyo.

In West Africa, the horrors of the slave trade continued until the 1860s. By that time, Catholic, Protestant, and Anglican missionaries had begun serious evangelization of Africa south of the Sahara. In Italy, post-Napoleonic France, and elsewhere, a new enthusiasm grew to promote missions. Religious congregations with a specifically African focus, such as the Holy Ghost Fathers, the Society of African Missions, the White Fathers, the Verona Fathers, and the Missionary Sisters of Verona, came into existence. Through the 20th century, with the dedication and help of African laymen and -women, Catholicism grew enormously in Africa. Despite the wounds of colonialism, recurrent wars, corrupt rulers, and famines, by the year 2000, 175 million out of 350 million Christians in Africa were Catholics. The first two African Catholics to become bishops of dioceses were appointed in 1939. By the year 1990, there were over 350 such African bishops, many of them concerned with the task of indigenizing or inculturating Catholic rituals in their region.

6. One of Mother Teresa's sisters looking after a dying patient

A last wave of Catholic missionary expansion that should be recalled affected North America, Oceania, and other parts of the globe. From the 19th century, congregations of missionary women began playing a major role in bringing Catholicism to such countries as Canada, the United States, Japan, Australia, and New Zealand. Along with numerous diocesan priests and men who belonged to religious communities, the Irish Sisters of Charity, Marist Sisters, Presentation Sisters, Religious of the Sacred Heart, Sisters of Mercy, and many other nuns founded schools, colleges, and hospitals around the world. They came from France, Germany, Ireland, Italy, and other European countries. The missionary activity of Nano Nagle (1718–84), St Rose Philippine Duchesne (1769–1852), Catherine Elizabeth McAuley (1778–1841), Mary Aikenhead (1787–1858), St Francis Xavier Cabrini (1850–1917), and their associates played a key role in creating world Catholicism. But this expansion of European Catholicism had hardly started before divisions arose at home – with the 16th-century Protestant Reformation.

The Reformation

At least since the Council of Vienne (1311–12), a cry for 'reform in head and members' was heard in the Catholic Church, as her life at various levels had become marked by many grave abuses. The situation was aggravated by the long absence from the diocese of Rome when the popes lived in Avignon (1309–77); the Great Western Schism (1378–1417), a period when eight popes and antipopes (those claiming to be Bishop of Rome in opposition to those held to be lawfully elected to that diocese) divided Western Christianity; and the Black Death, or bubonic plague, which suddenly arrived in 1346 and killed up to 20 million people, at least one-quarter of the European population. Europe did not reach its pre-plague level again until the 16th century began. The most generous priests, monks, and friars suffered disproportionately, since they went to the aid of the sick and dying. This loss of the best religious leadership played its part in

35

demoralizing the Church and society. The scandalous lives of such Renaissance popes as Alexander VI, who secured his own election largely through bribes and devoted much of his papal energies to furthering the position of his children, made reformation a crying need.

Judgements over the health or sickness of the Catholic Church in different countries still vary greatly. What, for example, was the situation like in England on the eve of the Reformation? Was the official church there well organized and meeting the spiritual needs of ordinary people? Eamon Duffy and others have challenged the conventional picture of a dysfunctional Catholicism in radical need of reform. But the debate still continues about the state of English faith before Henry VIII (king of England 1509–47) broke with the papacy and seized the monasteries and their property. The vigour of 16th-century Catholicism in Spain has come to be more widely recognized. Cardinal Ximenez de Cisneros (d. 1517) reformed the religious orders and encouraged the new learning. Among other contributions, he commissioned the first polyglot Bible of modern times, a six-volume work with parallel texts in Hebrew, Greek, and Latin. The monarchy controlled ecclesiastical affairs, insisted on a uniform religious-political orthodoxy, and helped make Spain an intensely Catholic society. Scholarship flourished, with Dominican theologians and philosophers leading the way. One of them, Francisco de Vitoria (d. 1546), developed a theory of international law that has proved lastingly important. Dominicans, Franciscans, and Jesuits provided an army of missionaries for evangelizing the New World. Mystics, such as St John of the Cross (d. 1591), St Teresa of Avila (d. 1582), and St Ignatius Loyola (d. 1556), left their mark on the whole Christian world through their lives and writing.

In the Low Countries, Erasmus of Rotterdam (d. 1536), through his *Praise of Folly* (1509), satirized the scandalous abuses he witnessed in the life of monasteries and of the Church at large. But

Thomas à Kempis (d. 1471) had lived in the same part of Europe and composed the extraordinarily popular *Imitation of Christ*, a text that described for all ages what a life centred on Jesus involves.

The start of the Protestant Reformation, often simply and better called the Reformation, is traditionally dated to 1517 when Martin Luther (1483–1546) produced his 95 theses in protest against the scandalous sale of indulgences and other abuses of papal and clerical power. The official church granted 'indulgences', or remissions of punishment in purgatory, for sinners who had repented of their sins but had died without making full satisfaction for the harm they had caused. On the authority of Pope Leo X, indulgences were being sold to raise money from the German faithful to help pay for the building of the new St Peter's Basilica in Rome. Luther felt outraged not only at this squalid practice but also at the whole idea that Church leaders could exercise control over the fate of human beings in the afterlife.

Intensely concerned with being justified by Christ ('Where do I find a gracious God who will heal the wounds of my guilt-stricken conscience?'), Luther argued for justification through divine grace alone (*sola gratia*), by faith alone (*sola fide*), and not by good works. He understood the Bible, and not human traditions, to be the only authoritative rule for faith (*sola scriptura*), and spread knowledge of the scriptures by translating the Bible into German. He also introduced the vernacular for the celebration of the Eucharist, demanded that lay people should receive Communion 'under both kinds' (that is, both the consecrated bread *and* wine), defended the right of clergy to marry, and opposed the authority of the pope.

Among the plethora of Protestant groups that emerged at the Reformation, some were extreme, even anarchical, but others were committed to clear ideas and precise ecclesiastical order. Jean

Calvin (1509–64) promoted this style of Reformation in France, Switzerland, and elsewhere. In his commentaries on the scriptures and his *Institutes* (first edition 1536), he showed himself a more rigorous theologian than Luther and more aware of the importance of organization. Presbyterianism, the form of church government created by Calvin, involves rule through a series of courts, up to the General Assembly – with the representative ministers and elders participating after being elected.

Undoubtedly, nationalism and economic interests helped the cause of the Reformation. But it was a deeply felt religious movement that aimed to purify church life and base Christian existence on the scriptures. Luther and Calvin expressed complementary emphases of perennial theological importance. Where Luther's call for reform was more oriented towards human beings who hear and believe the word of God, Calvin highlighted the majesty of God who elects the predestined and gives them the grace of obedient faith. In the 20th century, the Second Vatican Council (1962–5) was to acknowledge frankly 'that continued reformation' to which Christ always calls his Church (*Unitatis Redintegratio*, 6) – a confession that converged with the Reformers' sense of the enduring power of sin that constantly threatens communion with God.

Nevertheless, despite their appropriate respect for Calvin, Luther, and other leading Reformers, Catholics drew some lines: for instance, against Luther's notion of the human will being simply 'captive' to evil. A renowned Catholic scholar and friend of Thomas More (d. 1535), Erasmus in his *On Free Will* (1524), while respecting the sovereignty of God's grace and action, defended the free will of human beings. Erasmus's edition of the New Testament in Greek (1516) proved not only a landmark for biblical scholarship but also expressed his desire to reform Christian life in the light of the scriptures. But like the Catholic bishops at the reforming Council of Trent (1545–63), Erasmus did not agree that sin had so corrupted human beings that they could not freely exercise their wills when responding to the initiative of God's gifts. Nor did he accept division in Christendom as the price of badly needed reform.

Meeting over three periods for a total of 18 years, the Council of Trent remains the longest council in the history of the Catholic Church. Held in the northern Italian city of Trent, it was the culmination of a movement for Catholic renewal that pre-dated Luther. The first eight sessions (1545–7) did, however, treat such major themes raised by the Reformers as the relationship between scripture and tradition, justification, original sin, and the sacraments. Tensions between Emperor Charles V and the Pope led to a suspension of the Council, which eventually resumed for a second period (1551–2). The achievements of sessions nine to fourteen included decrees on the Eucharist and on the sacraments of penance (now called reconciliation) and extreme unction (now called anointing of the sick). After the new French king, Henry II, joined forces with some German princes who defeated Charles V and even threatened to overrun Trent, the Council was once again adjourned; it finally met again for a third period (1562–3). Its sessions fifteen to twenty-five defined doctrines about the Eucharist, the sacraments of orders and matrimony, and purgatory or purification after death from the effects of sin.

Trent brought a certain uniformity to the life of Western or Latin Catholics, with the standard Missal for Mass, the standard breviary (or book for daily prayer by priests and others), the Roman Catechism of 1566 (the first catechism published in the aftermath of any council), and the Sixto-Clementine Bible of 1592, the standard (Latin) text of the scriptures. Through its careful restatement and/or reformation of a whole range of beliefs and practices, the Council of Trent reshaped Catholicism up the end of the 18th century and even into the 20th century.

The Council led to the founding of seminaries, special colleges for the spiritual, intellectual, and pastoral training of candidates for the priesthood. St Charles Borromeo (1538–84), the influential archbishop of Milan, backed the foundation of seminaries. He encouraged the installation of altar rails in churches, which visibly expressed a division between the ordained priest who celebrated the Mass in the sanctuary and the baptized faithful who attended public worship in the nave, or central part of the church. Only a few churches built in earlier centuries had featured pulpits. New churches now regularly included prominent pulpits from which priests and bishops proclaimed Catholic doctrine. Religious orders sprang up and, through preaching, spiritual direction, and other ministries, aimed to renew Christian life. After being founded in 1540, the Jesuits quickly turned to education to spread faith and further the reformation of Christendom. By establishing colleges in many countries, they became known as 'the schoolmasters' of Europe and the New World.

Trent sealed a parting of the ways between Catholics and Protestants. In a prophetic mode, Protestants had denounced the worldliness and downright corruption of Catholicism and rightly championed the scriptures as the sacred norm for Christian life. But they reduced the sacramental mediation of God's grace to baptism and the Eucharist. By maintaining the seven sacraments (baptism, confirmation, the Eucharist, penance or reconciliation of sinners, anointing of the sick, holy orders, and matrimony), the Catholic Church maintained a tradition that aimed at touching and blessing all dimensions of human life. In the 18th century, Dr Samuel Johnson (1709–84) expressed this difference. Old, ill, and saddened by the thought of dying, he declared in the last summer of his life:

> A good man of a timorous disposition, in great doubt of his acceptance with God, and pretty credulous, may be glad of a church where there are so many helps to get to heaven. I would be a Papist, if I could. I have fear enough, but an obstinate rationality prevents me.

Even before the Council of Trent closed in 1563, the religious map of Europe was being redrawn. When Elizabeth I succeeded to the throne in 1558, England definitively ceased to be in communion with the bishop of Rome. The Church of England became an attractive third choice, alongside Catholicism and Protestantism.

Under the leadership of bishops in communion with the archbishop of Canterbury, Anglicanism understood itself to maintain the mainstream tradition of early Christianity, to be faithful to the scriptures, and to provide a middle road between papal authority and Protestant reform.

Jesuits became deeply involved in the struggle to save Austria, England, Germany, Poland, Scotland, and other countries for the one Catholic Church. But before the 16th century ended, not only England, Scotland, and Wales, but also parts of Germany and the Low Countries, Scandinavia, and some cantons of Switzerland had broken away from Catholicism. The political dimension of religious differences culminated in the Thirty Years War (1618–48), which weakened Spain, strengthened France, and devastated Germany. Hostilities ended in 1648 with two treaties forming the Peace of Westphalia; it endorsed the principle of '*cuius regio eius religio*', roughly translated as 'the government of a state determines its religious adherence'. This peace settlement extended protection to most religious minorities (whether Protestants in Catholic states or vice versa). Innocent X (pope 1644–55) denounced the treaties of Westphalia in a papal bull, but was universally ignored.

The new learning

Just as reform movements pre-dated Luther's protests, so too did the growth of new learning and thinking. Fifteenth-century Florence, universities across Europe, religious orders, rulers, and other individuals such as Johannes Gutenberg (d. 1468) fostered a new literacy and learning that shaped the world in which Catholics lived and thought. In the 2nd century AD, printing had begun in China, but geographical separation and, later, the opposition of Islam prevented this development from reaching Europe. In 1450, Gutenberg, a Mainz blacksmith, created a movable typeface of identical letters and invented what we know as the printing press. A vast new reading public grew up; mass literacy was on the way. Gutenberg made possible the new humanism of such figures as Erasmus, his friends Thomas More and John Colet (d. 1519) in England, and Charitas Pirckheimer (d. 1532) in Nuremberg. Benedictines, Dominicans, and other religious orders, both old and new, played an active role in spreading literacy and learning.

In the post-Gutenberg world, Catholics and others had many things to learn and to question. The new learning, no less than the discovery of other continents and the Reformation, challenged old certainties. Was monarchy God's chosen form of government, so that it would always be sinful to rebel against a monarch? Or could one agree with the Jesuit Juan Mariana (1536–1624) and justify in certain circumstances the killing of a tyrant? Was St Robert Bellarmine (1542–1621) correct in opposing the 'divine right of kings' and in holding that popes enjoyed only indirect, not direct, power in temporal matters? Could and should the state be used to enforce Church requirements?

More than a century later, over in North America, Charles Carroll (1737–1832) became the only Catholic among 55 signatories of the American Declaration of Independence (1776). During the colonial era, Catholics had been almost everywhere a despised and victimized minority. Along with his cousin, Archbishop John Carroll of Baltimore (1736–1815), who was the first Catholic bishop in the United States and the founder of Georgetown University (Washington, DC), Charles Carroll came to symbolize American religious freedom and a sense that the Catholic faith could and should be reconciled with the best features of the new, democratic political order.

The European union of altar and throne, which reached back to Emperor Constantine and was widely considered the norm for Catholic life, came to a grinding halt when the furies raged in the French Revolution. The Reign of Terror (1793–4) targeted clergy and religious men and women along with aristocrats, while the revolutionary government, with genocidal fervour, slaughtered devout peasants in the Vendée. When Napoleon had Pius VI (pope 1775–99) carried off as a prisoner to France, he took the Catholic Church to the edge. The troubles of the French Revolution unhinged papal power and prestige, and reduced the Catholic Church in France to its weakest state for over a thousand years.

But in post-Napoleonic France and beyond, Catholicism enjoyed a dramatic resurgence. New religious congregations of men and women, often with a missionary commitment, sprang up. Old and new devotions flowered: such as veneration of the Sacred Heart of Jesus and the use of the 'miraculous medal' which carried the image of the Virgin Mary. After the 1858 visions of St Bernadette Soubirous (1844–79), Lourdes became a place of pilgrimage for millions. Blessed Frédéric Ozanam (1813–53) founded in 1833 the Society of St Vincent de Paul, which continues to serve the needs of poor people.

Catholic teaching and scholarly life remained, however, at a low level, and did not match the developments in practice. Before and after Napoleon, Catholics and other Christians faced a serious challenge from the Enlightenment, the first major intellectual movement in the Western world for well over a thousand years to develop outside the control of the Catholic Church. Started in 17th-century Europe and then spread to the Americas, it resisted authority and tradition, championed human rights, encouraged empirical methods in scientific research, and aimed at deciding issues through the use of reason alone. Many personages of the Enlightenment rejected miracles and special divine revelation, and could be strongly opposed to official Christianity.

Some positive responses to the Enlightenment, both to its aberrations and to the critical thought it encouraged, came from figures like John Henry Newman (1801–90) and the founder of modern Catholic biblical studies, Marie-Joseph Lagrange (1855–1938). In a major document, the First Vatican Council (1869/70) defended a proper collaboration between faith (the response to divine revelation) and reason in all its forms. Leo XIII (pope 1878–1903) reacted to industrial urbanization and the huge social problems that ensued by defending the rights of workers in his ground-breaking encyclical of 1891, *Rerum novarum* ('of new things'). He drew on a German pioneer of Catholic social teaching, Bishop William Emmanuel von Ketteler (1811–77), and found much support from Cardinal Henry Edward Manning (1808–92) who dedicated himself to improving social conditions for workers in England and Ireland. An Austrian abbot, Johann Gregor Mendel (1822–84), through his experiments with peas in the monastery garden, demonstrated the primary source of variability in plants and animals and became the father of modern genetics.

But, in general, reactionary and closed attitudes prevailed well into the 20th century. Despite some attractive features of his papacy, Pius IX (pope 1846–78) epitomizes this resistance. In the 80 propositions of his *Syllabus of Errors* (1964), he published a comprehensive attack on 'modern errors'. Besides condemning views that most Christians would reject (such as 'any action of God on human beings and the world must be denied', and 'faith in Christ is detrimental to human reason'), he also reasserted the temporal power of popes and opposed freedom of speech and religion. He used public executions in an attempt to maintain civil order right up to 1870, when the papal states fell and the forces of united Italy entered Rome. Although the 19th century saw the emancipation of Jews in most countries, in 1850 Pius IX reinstated in the city the closed ghetto for Jews and introduced anti-Jewish legislation. At a time when slavery was being abolished, he argued that it could be reconciled with divine revelation and the natural law.

Pius IX died in 1878, exactly one century before the election of John Paul II, a pope who rejected the death penalty, repeatedly asked pardon for the wrongs Catholics have committed against Jews, and worked hard to further dialogue between the Catholic Church and other Christian bodies. During the pontificate of Pio Nono, John Paul II would have been gaoled in Castel San Angelo for saying, writing, and doing such things. At the end of the 20th century, his international impact depended in part on something Pius IX could not imagine: namely, freedom from the burden and limitation of governing a sovereign country, the papal states.

The end of Pius IX's long pontificate witnessed struggles with hostile states: for instance, in Germany the anti-Catholic campaign led by Otto von Bismarck that reached its height in 1871–5, and the pressure on the Church from anticlerical governments in France after 1870. Such Church–state conflicts grew more violent in the 20th century: the killing of almost 7,000 priests and the destruction of hundreds of churches during the Spanish Civil War (1936–9) that ended with General Franco's ruthless suppression of his opponents; the persecution of many Catholics and other Christians in Nazi Germany (1933–45), along with the complicity of many Catholics and other Christians in Hitler's crimes; persecutions, under European Communism (down to 1989) and under Chinese Communism (since 1949); and endemic violence and oppression in some Muslim-dominated states.

The coming of the world church

How can we sum up the situation of Catholicism at the end of the 20th century, one marked by the immense and murderous catastrophes of two world wars? It proved a bloodstained century, with 55 million being killed or starving to death during the Second World War (1939–45) alone.

One act of wilful murder stands out: the Shoah. Adolf Hitler and his collaborators systematically exterminated nearly six million European Jews. After Rolf Hochhuth attacked Pius XII (pope 1939–58) in a play *The Deputy: A Christian Tragedy* (1963), it became popular to accuse Pius XII of failure to challenge the Nazis publicly over their dreadful murder of Jews. Books and articles have poured out from such authors as James Carroll, Daniel Goldhagen, Robert Katz, Steven T. Katz, and Susan Zuccotti, with the grounds for attack often shifting over the years from 'he was indifferent to Jewish suffering in the Holocaust' (Hochhuth) to 'he was not as concerned about Nazi efforts to exterminate Jews as he should have been' (John Cornwell in *Hitler's Pope* (1999)). An indispensable source for scholars working on the issue are the 11 volumes of documents from the Vatican archives that cover the period of the Second World War (published by Pierre Blet and his fellow historians up to 1981). In contrast, numerous writers have defended and praised Pius XII for all that he did to save Jews. They include such figures as an Anglican historian, Owen Chadwick, who established that Pius XII was party to a plot against Hitler in the winter of 1939/40, and a Jewish professor of history and political science, David G. Dalin, whose 2005 study answers the case brought by Carroll, Cornwell, and others. Without having done the historical research necessary to adjudicate the debate competently, I always remain aware of the fact that when the Second World War ended, the chief rabbi of Rome became a Catholic and was baptized as 'Eugenio', the baptismal name of Pius XII. Eugenio Zolli then lived for a short time in a building in Rome where I also lived for over 30 years (1974–2006).

Along with Nazism, the Communism of Joseph Stalin (1879–1953) and of Mao Tse-Tung (1893–1976) marked the century until, at least in Europe, this ideology officially ended when the Berlin Wall came down in November 1989. The sudden collapse of the Soviet Union was perhaps the most surprising event in the entire century.

These and other dramatic changes affected the 20th-century story of Catholicism. In 1900, almost two-thirds of the world's Catholics lived in Europe and North America; by 1993, three-quarters of them lived in Latin America, Africa, and Asia. An even more startling demographic change came with the fact that, by the time the world population passed the six billion mark in October 1999, more than half the Catholics who have ever existed lived in the 20th century.

Another way of expressing the shift is to recall the conclave of cardinals who elected Paul VI (pope 1963–78); 65% of those cardinals were Europeans and more than one-third were Italians. By the time of the 1978 conclave that elected John Paul II, the Italian cardinals were down to one-quarter and those from Western Europe down to fewer than half. Beyond question, the Italians and Europeans were still over-represented in 1978, but a clear demographic change had come in the college of cardinals, and it was no accident that by electing John Paul II, they chose the first non-Italian pope in more than 400 years.

John Paul II as a Polish bishop had attended Vatican II, the first Ecumenical Council to show the universality of the Catholic Church. Even so, the Council manifested a trend rather than an achieved reality. For example, only 311 of the 2,600 Council Fathers came from Africa; of these 311, only 60 were Africans. Nevertheless, the Council showed how, within the Catholic Church and beyond, the old days of European hegemony were drawing to a close.

When the Council opened in October 1962, the Cuban Missile Crisis had brought the USA and the Soviet Union to the brink of a

7. Pope Paul VI and Dr Michael Ramsey, the Archbishop of Canterbury, in March 1966 sign a common declaration, which inaugurated an Anglican–Roman Catholic dialogue that they hoped would lead to unity in truth and faith

nuclear war. John XXIII (pope 1958–63), who had already called the Council, played a key role in defusing that crisis. A few months later, he published his plea for a new world order, *Pacem in Terris* ('Peace on Earth'). When he died in June 1963, some units of the Russian navy flew their flags at half-mast. In October 1965, a few weeks after the fourth session of Vatican II opened, Paul VI went to New York and addressed a message of peace ('Never again war') to the United Nations – being the first pope ever to speak to that body which represents the nations of the world.

Vatican II had a double aim: an *aggiornamento* (updating) of the Church's own life, worship, and teaching; and new relationships with other Christian communities, Jews, Muslims, and members of other world religions. The first and last of the documents issued by the Council express the double aim. Through *Sacrosanctum Concilium* (4 December 1963), the bishops endorsed the reform of Catholic worship by, firstly, a return to earlier and simpler forms, and secondly, the use of the vernacular or local language. The last and longest conciliar text, *Gaudium et Spes* (7 December 1965), spelled out the bishops' ideals and values for Christian and human life at the end of the second millennium. On the same day, Paul VI and the Orthodox Patriarch of Constantinople issued a joint declaration, expressing their regret for nine centuries of division and hopes for future reconciliation. Through ceremonies held simultaneously in the Vatican and at the Patriarch's residence in Istanbul, they lifted the mutual excommunications between the Orthodox and the Catholic Churches.

The Council has affected the lives of Catholics around the world in many ways: through the new rites for the administration of baptism and other sacraments; through closer relations with other Christians, Jews, and followers of different religions; through encouragement given to new forms of life consecrated to prayer and apostolic activity; through changes in the training of candidates for the ordained ministry; and through other smaller and larger changes. Many of the new directions are reflected in the 1983 Code of Canon Law (for the Western Church) and the 1990 Code of Canons of the Oriental Churches (for the Eastern Church). The Council also opened the way for developments on a scale scarcely imaginable to earlier Catholics. Let me mention a few examples.

First, the papacy. By continuing and enormously expanding the travels of Paul VI, John Paul II made the papacy a world presence by visiting almost every major nation and many smaller nations around the globe. Before he died on 2 April 2005, he had been out of Italy over 100 times on 'apostolic pilgrimages', which often included stops in several countries.

Also, since the close of Vatican II in 1965, the Church has experienced the rise of Catholic feminism, the work of various liberation theologians (who frequently looked back to Las Casas for their inspiration), and fresh attempts at dialogue with the great religions of Asia. At the end of this book we will come back to these and other trends and challenges.

Chapter 3
Catholics on God and the human condition

What are the beliefs about God and the human condition that hold together and shape the worldwide Catholic Church? Here, if anywhere, our answers reflect much common ground shared with Catholics by other Christians. All Christians endorse the Nicene-Constantinopolitan Creed (of 381), which summarizes faith in the tripersonal God, the incarnation of the Son of God, and the human path through baptism and the forgiveness of sins to life everlasting. Yet, even here, there are specific Catholic emphases and preferences that will be recalled below. Catholics have taken a broader view than some other Christians by drawing their account of God from the scriptures, public worship, personal experience, and philosophical reflection.

The Bible and its authority

From the time of Justin Martyr and Irenaeus of Lyon in the 2nd century, the whole Bible and the story it tells have always been acknowledged as the primary way of knowing God. When Catholics express faith in God, they mean the God of Abraham, Isaac, and Jacob, identified as the Father of Our Lord Jesus Christ, and known to the wide world through the outpouring of the Holy Spirit at the first Pentecost. It is the self-disclosure of God, along with the impact of this revelation, that is the primary theme of the Bible. To be sure, Catholics share the Old Testament belief that

God is also disclosed through the visible works of Creation. In the words of a psalm, 'the heavens proclaim the glory of God and the firmament shows forth the work of his hands' (Ps. 19: 1). But it is the special initiative of God conveyed through the history of the Old Testament and New Testament that has freely 'lifted the veil' on God and the divine plan for human beings.

Vatican II's 1965 Constitution on Divine Revelation (*Dei Verbum*) understands this disclosure to be primarily God's self-revelation, which invites the personal response of faith, and to be secondarily the communication of truths about God and human beings that would otherwise remain unknown. Thus *Dei Verbum* recognizes revelation to be firstly the personal manifestation of the divine Mystery (upper case) and secondly the disclosure of the divine mysteries (lower case) that were previously hidden from human knowledge and understanding. In revelation we primarily meet God and not divinely authorized truths. This understanding of God's self-manifestation entails presenting human faith as a matter of a total human response to the divine revelation. Far from being predominantly, or even exclusively, the mind accepting revealed truths, faith is the 'obedient' response of the whole person – head, heart, and actions – with the help of the Holy Spirit, to the self-manifestation of God (*Dei Verbum*, 5).

The self-revelation of God changes and even transforms human beings who hear the divine word and let themselves be opened up to God's self-manifestation. The Old Testament prophets appreciated how the divine words, so far from being merely informative statements, powerfully bring about results. God's word is like rain that causes germination, 'giving seed to the sower and bread to the eater' (Isa. 55: 10). God's revelation and saving activity may be distinguishable but are never separable; they belong together as the two sides of the loving self-communication of God. When Christ 'completes and perfects' the divine self-manifestation, he reveals that 'God is with us to liberate us from the darkness of sin and death and raise us up to eternal life'

(*Dei Verbum*, 4). In the language of John's Gospel, Christ is the saving 'Life' of the world because he is the revealing 'Light' of the world, and vice versa.

Vatican II presents revelation as utterly centred on Christ. In his incarnation, life, death, resurrection, and co-sending (with God the Father) of the Holy Spirit, Christ forms the climax of the divine self-revelation (ibid. 4, 17). As John's Gospel puts it, 'the Word became flesh and lived among us, and we have seen his glory, the glory of the Father's only Son. It is God the only Son, who is close to the Father's heart, who has made him known' (John 1: 14, 18).

In one sense, the Christ-event was and remains the fullness and completion of divine revelation. Having spoken and acted through the visible presence of his incarnate Son and the sending of the Spirit, God has nothing greater to say, nothing more to reveal, and no other agent of revelation who could match Christ. In that sense, the historical revelation through Christ is full, unparalleled and unsurpassable in principle. God can and will call up subordinate ministers and mediators of revelation, but they cannot be like Christ, either in kind or in degree. His divine identity puts him qualitatively beyond any possible 'rival' in the work of revelation (and salvation).

But in another sense, we do not yet enjoy the fullness and completion of revelation. The final vision of God is still to come. As St John puts it, 'Beloved, we are God's children now; what we will be has not yet been revealed. What we know is this: when he [God] is revealed, we will be like him, for we will see him as he is' (1 John 3: 2). As we wait in hope for this complete, saving revelation, we see and know only 'dimly' and not yet fully. Referring to the imperfect mirrors of his time, St Paul writes: 'Now we see in a mirror dimly, but then face to face. Now I know in part; then I shall understand fully, even as I have been fully understood' (1 Cor. 13: 12). Calling on the Letter to Titus 2: 13, Vatican II teaches that the 'glorious manifestation of our Lord,

Jesus Christ' is still to come (*Dei Verbum*, 4). The 'not yet' of this future manifestation qualifies the revelation 'already' brought by Christ and the Holy Spirit.

Besides the past and future aspects of revelation, *Dei Verbum* also portrays revelation as an ongoing reality which is ever being actualized and constantly invites human faith: 'The "obedience of faith" (Rom. 16: 26)...must be given to the God who reveals' (no. 5). People are called, in one generation after another, to accept in faith the divine self-manifestation that was completed with Jesus and his first disciples. *Dei Verbum* associates revelation as it happened *then* with revelation as it happens *now* in the Church: 'God, who spoke in the past, continues to converse with the spouse of his beloved Son' (no. 8). Vatican II's Constitution on the Sacred Liturgy (*Sacrosanctum Concilium*), when expounding the various ways Christ is present in the Church's public worship, acknowledges that 'it is he himself who speaks when the sacred scriptures are read in church'; in the context of worship, 'Christ is still proclaiming his gospel' (nos. 7, 33). Just as faith is a present event, so too is the light of divine self-revelation that comes through the Eucharist, the other sacraments, preaching, reading the scriptures, public and private prayer, and many other channels that summon forth faith.

In short, Catholic teaching portrays the revelation of God not only as reaching its unsurpassable climax in the past (with Jesus Christ) but also as a present and future event. We can express this triple time reference by distinguishing between the climax of 'foundational' revelation (which took place back in the 1st century AD), 'dependent' revelation (which is ceaselessly actualized now for those who hear God's revealing word), and 'final' revelation (which will be the definitive self-revelation of God at the end of history).

After its opening chapter on divine revelation, *Dei Verbum* moves in its second chapter to the question of *tradition*, understood to be both the process of 'handing on' (tradition as act) and the living heritage that is handed on (tradition as content). Both the process and the heritage are located within the believing community. The dynamic of tradition, both as act and as content, was already very much at work in the history of Israel, when the Jewish people handed on the memory of their sufferings and the powerful disclosure of God, who delivered them from slavery in Egypt and brought them home from exile in Babylon. Parents passed on to their children the marvellous story of the saving acts of God (Deut. 6: 20–5; 26: 5–10). Tradition was the setting for appropriating and understanding the revelation of God in their history.

With the outpouring of the Holy Spirit, the whole Church was empowered to transmit her memory, experience, and expression of the normative self-revelation of God that was completed with Christ and the New Testament community. Thus tradition involves the 'Church in her doctrine, life, and worship' transmitting to every generation 'all that she has, all that she believes' (*Dei Verbum*, 8). What then is the relationship between the inspired scriptures and the 'prior' and 'larger' realities of divine revelation and the Church in her 'transmitting' role?

As such, the scriptures are written testimonies which, after the history of divine revelation had begun, came into existence under the inspiration of the Holy Spirit and through the work of some believers at various stages in the foundational history of God's people. Thus the scriptures differ from revelation in the way that written texts differ from living, interpersonal events. It makes perfectly good sense to say with exasperation: 'I left my copy of the Bible behind in the London Underground.' But I would have a good deal of explaining to do if I were to say to a friend, 'I left revelation behind in the Underground.'

As an inspired text, the Bible illuminates for millions of Catholics and other Christians the deepest reality of God and human beings; it is indispensable for Christian existence, both collectively and individually. Nevertheless, revelation or the living word of God remains a broader reality and is not limited to the Bible and its immediate impact. God's living word is not confined to a written text, even one written under the special guidance of the Holy Spirit.

Eventually, the inspired books were acknowledged for their unique authority and formed the *canon* of scripture, a closed list of texts that is normative for Catholic life and practice. A 1546 decree from the Council of Trent definitively established the biblical canon for Catholics. But the process of 'canonization' had begun in the early centuries of Christianity. As we saw in Chapter 1, Irenaeus upheld, on the one hand, the unique value of the New Testament scriptures, especially the Gospels according to Matthew, Mark, Luke, and John, against Gnostic attempts to add further 'gospels' and other texts. On the other hand, he defended the enduring authority of the Old Testament scriptures against Marcion's total rejection of them.

Concretely what are the canonical books of the Catholic Bible? *The Oxford Annotated Bible* prints first 39 books of the Old Testament, then 7 books (plus sections of books) under the heading of 'Apocryphal/Deuterocanonical' books (books composed or translated into Greek some time after 200 BC), and at the end the 27 books of the New Testament. 'Deuterocanonical' is the Catholic name for those 7 books (Tobit, Judith, Wisdom, Sirach or Ecclesiasticus, Baruch, and 1 and 2 Maccabees) plus further portions of other books, found in the Greek or Septuagint version of the Old Testament but not in the canon of Hebrew scriptures that emerged in the 2nd century AD. Protestants have normally called these writings 'Apocrypha' ('hidden' or 'not genuine') and have tended not to include them in their Bibles. When Catholics and Orthodox believers speak of the 'deuterocanonical' ('of the second canon') books of the Bible, they do not intend a negative judgement, as if these books were less important or less inspired. The term refers rather to the fact that debates preceded their securing a permanent place in the canon. 'Deuterocanonical' also

Catholicism

suggests the fact that the books in question were composed (or translated into Greek) at the end of the Old Testament period: that is to say, after the composition of the other Old Testament books.

The tripersonal God

When asked 'What is God like?', Catholics, along with other Christians, point to the scriptures, both the Old Testament and the New Testament. The first disciples of Jesus and early Christians maintained their inherited Jewish faith in one God (monotheism), but did so in the light of the life, death, and resurrection of Jesus (together with the outpouring of the Holy Spirit). Without abandoning Jewish monotheism, they came to accept a 'differentiated' monotheism that maintained 'one God' but distinguished within the Godhead between Father, Son, and Holy Spirit, as we see in the baptismal formula at the end of Matthew's Gospel (Matt. 28: 19). Since the Trinitarian faith of early Christianity identified YHWH (or 'Yahweh', the God of Israel) as the Father of Our Lord Jesus Christ (Eph. 1: 3, 17), we need to recall the antecedent Jewish faith in God.

Jewish faith grew through a long history of personal and collective encounters with God: from such shadowy figures as Abraham, Sarah, Melchizedek, and others who belonged to the patriarchal period (that lasted down to around 1200 BC), who are gratefully remembered in the New Testament (e.g. Rom. 4: 1–25; Hebr. 5–7), and two of whom (Abraham and Melchizedek) are recalled in the First Eucharistic Prayer (or ancient 'Roman Canon' of the Latin rite), right down to Mary, Joseph, Elizabeth, Zachariah, Simeon, and Anna – those holy men and women who people Luke's account of Jesus' conception and birth (Luke 1–2).

From these chapters of Luke's Gospel, Catholics and other Christians have drawn some very Jewish prayers that have constantly nourished their faith in God and vision of God: the

Magnificat (from the words of Mary), the *Benedictus* (from Zachariah), the *Nunc Dimittis* (from Simeon) – not to mention the *Gloria in Excelsis Deo* inspired by the angelic praise when Christ was born (Luke 2: 14) and the *Ave Maria*, or *Hail Mary*, inspired by words addressed to Mary by the angel Gabriel and Elizabeth (Luke 1: 28, 42). To be sure, Catholic and Christian faith in God has been nourished even more by the Lord's Prayer (Matt. 6: 9–13). But the vision of God Jesus conveyed in that prayer is, for the most part, deeply rooted in the Old Testament.

Dramatic moments punctuated the long Jewish experience of salvation history. God appeared to Moses in a 'flame of fire' that came out of a blazing bush in the wilderness, presenting himself as 'the God of Abraham, Isaac, and Jacob' and revealing the divine name of YHWH, interpreted as 'I am who I am' or 'I will be who I will be'. God commissioned Moses to liberate the chosen people from their captivity in Egypt (Exod. 3: 1–4: 17). Their deliverance involved not only 40 years of wandering in the desert but also God's covenant at Mount Sinai, pre-eminent among the seven covenants gratefully recalled by Ben Sira (Sir. 44–7). From the outset, Christians understood the resurrection to embody and effect a new exodus from the slavery of sin and death, and the Eucharist to 're-present' the new covenant with God that Jesus instituted at the Last Supper.

Traditionally ascribed to King David, the psalms formed the hymnal of ancient Israel and seem to have been mostly composed to accompany acts of worship in the magnificent Temple constructed in Jerusalem by David's son and successor, King Solomon. The psalms reflected the people's deeply personal experience of God, as they joyfully praised YHWH, asked for help in time of trouble, expressed confidence in the divine power, and, both collectively and individually, poured out their hearts to their God. The psalms became the prayerbook for Catholic Christianity, used day after day by communities and individuals in their public and private worship. For 2,000 years, the psalms have shaped and interpreted the sense that Catholics and other Christians have of who God is and what God does.

Over the centuries, Catholics have learned more of God from using the psalms in prayer than from studying the teaching of general councils of the Church. Philosophical thinking shaped this teaching, as when the Fourth Lateran Council (1215) confessed 'the one true God' to be 'eternal, immense [i.e. being unmeasured and unmeasurable], unchangeable, incomprehensible, almighty, ineffable', and 'entirely simple'. To this list the First Vatican Council (1869/70) added a few such attributes as God being 'infinite in intellect, will, and all perfection'. These precise adjectives can keep errors at bay. More importantly, the boundlessly intense nature of these attributes (God as in-finite, im-mense, and un-changeable, and therefore for us in-comprehensible and in-effable) respects the mysterious otherness of the divine Being who largely transcends human knowing. The central prayers of Catholic Christianity – the Lord's Prayer, the *Benedictus*, the *Magnificat*, the *Gloria in Excelsis Deo* – and the Nicene-Constantinopolitan Creed, have more to say about what God does (for example, in creating all things, forgiving sins, and 'lifting up the lowly') than about what God is like (for example, as almighty and sovereign Lord).

Their religious experience led the Israelites to develop an image of God that combined in a remarkable way *majesty transcendence* and *loving closeness*. God was the utterly mysterious 'Other', three times acclaimed as holy by heavenly creatures (Isa. 6: 3). But God was also tenderly close to his people like a loving parent or spouse (e.g. Hos. 11: 3–4). Both this otherness and this closeness fed into the Catholic (and Christian) sense of God. On the one hand, as the *Sanctus* or *Trisagion*, the thrice holy acclaim of God passed into the worship of Catholics (and other Christians); in every eucharistic prayer the *Sanctus* follows the preface. On the other hand, Jesus' sense of God being lovingly present as 'Abba', or 'Father dear', profoundly characterized his religious experience and preaching, and became the standard (but not exclusive) name for the first person of the divine Trinity.

It was Jesus who triggered the development from Jewish to Christian monotheism, or belief in one God now distinguished into *three persons*. At least implicitly, Jesus claimed an authority and personal identity on a par with God. One can understand why some religious leaders rejected Jesus' claims as blasphemous and incompatible with their strict monotheism. After his resurrection from the dead, the earliest Christians recognized and proclaimed Jesus to be not just a wonderful human being vindicated by God but the only Son of God and their divine Lord.

In the opening greetings of his letters, St Paul, the first Christian author, set 'the Lord Jesus Christ' side by side with 'God our Father' as the source of 'grace and peace' – that is to say, of integral salvation. In a hymn that the apostle composed or, more likely, took over from early Christian worship (Phil. 2: 6–11), he attributed to Jesus 'equality with God', as well as the right to bear the divine name of 'Lord' and so receive adoration from the whole universe. A 'Trinitarian' farewell rounded off the final chapter of the apostle's Second Letter to the Corinthians: 'The grace of our Lord Jesus Christ and the love of God and the fellowship of the Holy Spirit be with you all' (2 Cor. 13: 13). Here 'the Lord Jesus Christ' was set alongside God [the Father] and the Holy Spirit.

After experiencing the risen Jesus, the first Christians and then Paul followed him in praying to God as 'Abba'. Paul and other New Testament Christians knew themselves to enjoy their adopted status as God's sons and daughters through the Holy Spirit whom they had received (Rom. 8: 14–17; Gal. 4: 4–7). Thus Christians, while continuing to be monotheistic by maintaining faith in the one God (e.g. Gal. 3: 20), now included in their new form of monotheism Christ the Son of God and the Holy Spirit. They expressed this faith by baptizing 'in the name [singular] of the Father and of the Son and of the Holy Spirit' (Matt. 28: 19). This tripartite formula did not offer anything like the later, full-blown doctrine of God as three in one and one in three. Admittedly, it implied a unity ('the name'), distinction, and equality between the Father, the Son, and the Holy Spirit. Yet the formula did not clarify such matters as their mutual relations. It provided, nevertheless, a foundation and starting point for confessing and expounding the Trinity and shaped profoundly Catholic worship.

Catholics (and many other Christians) invoke the Trinity when they sign themselves with the cross on their forehead, breast, and shoulders. The celebration of the Eucharist opens 'in the name of the Father, and of the Son, and of the Holy Spirit'; it closes with a blessing that calls on the Trinity. During the Eucharist, as well as in other liturgical ceremonies, the collects or variable prayers end by invoking the Trinity. In the divine office, the official prayer used by priests, religious, and many lay people, the canticles and psalms conclude with a doxology or praise of the Trinity: 'Glory be to the Father and to the Son and to the Holy Spirit, as it was in the beginning, is now, and ever shall be, world without end. Amen.' In the sacrament of penance, the priest pronounces words of absolution that are thoroughly Trinitarian:

> God, the Father of mercies, through the death and resurrection of his Son, has reconciled the world to himself and sent the Holy Spirit among us for the forgiveness of sins; through the ministry of the Church may God give you pardon and peace, and I absolve you from your sins in the name of the Father, and of the Son, and of the Holy Spirit.

For Catholics and other Christians, the 'law' of public worship has never ceased to indicate the central 'law' of belief: faith in the tripersonal God. Like Paul's teaching on Father, Son, and Holy Spirit, the liturgical usage is not abstract or philosophical. It draws on the scriptures and remains firmly situated within the context of salvation and the experience of the baptized.

When encouraging Catholics to prepare for the Jubilee Year of 2000 and the coming third millennium, John Paul II swept aside suggestions about seven years of preparation, one for each of the seven sacraments. In his 1994 apostolic letter *Tertio Millennio Adveniente* ('As the third millennium approaches'), he went to the Trinitarian heart of the matter by inviting all Christians to dedicate in a special way 1997 to Jesus Christ, 1998 to the Holy Spirit, and 1999 to God the Father.

Those who wish to know what Catholics believe about the Trinity could well be advised to attend some church services, preferably in both the Eastern and Western rites. By listening carefully to the prayers and hymns, and by contemplating the icons and other images, they may come close to appreciating what faith in the tripersonal God means in the great scheme of things to rank-and-file Catholic believers.

One could dedicate many more pages to other questions: about the Holy Spirit (such as the need for Western Catholics to develop a more vibrant sense of the Holy Spirit) and about Christ (in particular, an account of what is lost by those who deny his true divinity or reduce his full humanity). Limits of space require leaving all this to further reading.

Human beings: created, sinful, and redeemed

Catholics share with other Christians a faith in God, the 'Maker of all things, visible and invisible' (Nicene-Constantinopolitan Creed). Through creation, the sovereign divine freedom brought about a reality that differs from God and yet constantly and totally depends upon God. While always radically 'beyond' and 'other', God is so intimately present, especially to human beings, that St Augustine of Hippo could say to God in his *Confessions*: 'you were more inward than my inmost self" – or, as some translate these words, 'you were closer to me than I was to myself' (3.6).

God created man and woman in the divine image and likeness (Gen. 1: 26), so as to have, as Irenaeus put it, someone on whom to shower the divine gifts. In richly symbolic language, the opening chapters of Genesis tell the story of the creation of 'Adam' and 'Eve' and their fall into sin. They transgressed the divine command, ate the forbidden fruit, and lost both their innocent relationship with each other and their trusting relationship with God. Far from enhancing their existence, sin left 'the man' and 'the woman' less than what they should have been and ushered in destructive consequences.

The most distressing consequence is death. Fashioned from dust (Gen. 2: 7), the man and the woman are by nature mortal. Their death should have been like that of Abraham, who was to die surrounded by his family in 'ripe old age' – a death that peacefully completed a life spent in faithful obedience to God (Gen. 25: 1–11). But disobedience to God has changed the experience of death for sinful human beings; death has become a troubling fate (Gen. 3: 19), a distressing sign of sin. Flanked by suffering and pain, death signals the radical change sin has brought to the human condition.

The opening chapters of Genesis present the sinfulness that emerged at humanity's origins as an enduring legacy of evil, which would be expressed in terms of inherited *original sin* and deliberate personal sin. For Pelagius (a scholar from the British Isles who came to Rome in the late 4th century) and his followers, the sin of Adam had not interiorly harmed his descendants and, in particular, had left quite intact the natural use of their free will. Human beings can achieve salvation through their own sustained efforts. Augustine resisted the Pelagians on several grounds. First, the long-standing practice of baptizing infants, and doing so for the remission of sins, meant that infants come into the world with some kind of inherited sinful state. They are born deprived of the life of grace that they would have possessed but for Adam's sin. Second, since God sent his Son to save the whole of humanity, everyone must somehow be under the reign of sin and in need of Christ and baptism. Third, as a consequence of Adam's sin, the freedom of human beings remains deeply impaired, though not destroyed; we constantly need God's grace to share in the redemption brought by Christ. At no stage is salvation a 'do-it-yourself' affair.

The 16th-century leaders of the Protestant Reformation re-opened the question of 'original sin', but at the other extreme from any Pelagian optimistic minimalizing of the damage caused by the fall of Adam and Eve. For Luther, Calvin, and others, the sin of our first parents totally corrupted human beings and destroyed their freedom. Luther, in particular, identified human 'concupiscence', or disordered desire, as a direct consequence of Adam's fall and an irresistible inclination that persists even after baptism. In a decree on 'original sin' (1546), the Council of Trent accepted that concupiscence remains in the baptized but only as an 'inclination to sin', not 'sin in the true and proper sense'. The Council echoed the view of the *Exultet*, an ancient hymn of praise sung during the Easter Vigil, which, without using the term 'original sin', calls it 'the happy fault' that merited for us human beings such a Saviour.

Hence 'original sin' refers not only to human solidarity in sin but also, and even more, to the call to a new, supernatural life in Christ. Far from being merely a depressing statement about the wounded or deficient nature of the inherited human condition, the doctrine of original sin underlines humanity's need for Christ's grace; there is no way to true fulfilment and eternal life except through him.

In the primary and proper sense of the word, sin is always personal, a freely committed offence against a loving God for which the sinner must take responsibility and ask forgiveness.

Sin means allowing oneself to become enslaved, corrupting one's human dignity and environment, and succumbing to an egotistical love of oneself, associated with a deep unwillingness to love God and one's fellow human beings. The salvation brought by Christ provides the remedy for this threefold evil of sin. He delivers sinners from the power of evil; he expiates or cleanses the defilement of sin; his love reconciles human beings to God and to one another.

Through the totally gratuitous gift of God, sinful human beings can enjoy the unmerited favour of being justified and saved in Christ through faith (Rom. 3: 24–5). They can be reborn (John 1: 13; 3: 3) and share in the new life of grace (Eph. 2: 4-6). This new life means becoming adopted children of God, brothers and sisters of the risen Christ, and 'temples' indwelt by the Holy Spirit (Rom. 8: 12–17; 1 Cor. 3: 16). This intimate sharing in the life of the Trinity (2 Pet. 1: 3-4) will be consummated beyond death through the immediate vision of God in the final kingdom. Thus the life of grace entails the hope of glory.

The Catholic *doctrine of grace* emerged from two great controversies. In the 4th and 5th centuries, the Pelagians (along with their later successors) stressed self-sufficient freedom, as if human beings were able to achieve salvation through their own resources. Against this, Augustine and his successors insisted that, from start to finish, human beings rely on the initiative of God's loving grace if they are to be saved.

In the 16th century, the major Reformers held that human nature has been so deeply corrupted by 'original sin' that we remain steeped in sinfulness and commit sin in every action. Luther and Calvin used strong, even lurid, language about human depravity. But there is room for a generous reading that seems closer to what the Reformers intended. The closer human beings draw to God in their spiritual lives, the more they will become aware of and even terrified by the overwhelming divine holiness that rises infinitely above our tainted and limited nature. Responding to the Reformers in 1547, the Council of Trent agreed on the utter primacy of divine grace in the whole process of human justification and salvation. By their own free will, human beings cannot 'take one step towards justice in God's sight'. They must always be 'awakened and assisted by divine grace, if they are to repent of their sins and be reborn through baptism'. At the same time, the grace received in baptism interiorly transforms sinners. Through the strength constantly imparted by Christ, those who have been justified can and should perform good works that merit for them eternal life. They can freely cooperate with God's grace and do not necessarily 'sin in all their works'. What Trent taught here corresponds to a central conviction of Augustine: God crowns our merits, but, in doing so, he is in fact crowning his gifts.

Christ as fulfilment

The life of glory that the life of grace initiates is centred on the final coming of Christ in glory, the ultimate gift of God to human beings. Catholics have traditionally spoken of the 'last things', the first being death itself. A specifically Catholic understanding of death can be gleaned primarily from the rites for the dying, from prayers written for Masses on behalf of the deceased, from burial rites, and from inscriptions on tombs. The conviction that 'life is changed, not taken away' characterizes this attitude towards death. Catholics (and other Christians) face death with a hope centred on the risen and living Christ. At funeral Masses, the presence of the great Easter candle near the coffin illustrates this hope. Christ, who has been the dead person's light and life since baptism, will continue to be that light now that the deceased is born into never-ending life.

With death, the history of each person assumes its complete, irreversible character, and is 'judged' by God in what came to be called the 'particular judgement'. At death, individuals know their condition in relationship with God. But are they all ready for the face-to-face vision of God that will bring them eternal happiness? Realizing that many deceased needed first to be cleansed (through Christ's merits) from the effects of their sins in a state that would be called 'purgatory', from early times Christians prayed to God for the dead and celebrated the Eucharist for them. On her deathbed, St Monica (d. 387) asked Augustine and her other son to 'remember her at the altar of God'.

After such post-mortem purification (or immediately, if this is not needed), those who die in the love of God are gifted with an immediate and eternal vision of the tripersonal God. They dwell with God and enjoy the utterly fulfilling vision of the infinitely good and beautiful God. As the 1992 *Catechism of the Catholic Church* puts it, there will be 'the blessed community of all who are perfectly incorporated in Christ' (no. 1026).

If such glory awaits the blessed in heaven, what of people who definitively close themselves to God's saving love? Hell (as a state of permanent and painful separation from God) remains a possibility for those who through deliberate malice refuse to love God and their neighbour (see Matt. 25: 31–46). With death their choice is sealed forever. But, as John Paul II taught (in 1999), one does not know 'whether or which human beings are found in hell'. Catholics (and other Christians) may and should pray that this terrible possibility will never be realized for anyone. Jesus left terrifying warnings about the possible outcome of serious sin. Yet Catholics may hope that the divine purpose to save everyone will be effective (1 Tim. 2: 3–6) and that, finally, God will be 'all in all' (1 Cor. 15: 28).

When Jesus comes in glory at the 'general judgement', the whole of humanity will definitively know the truth about itself. Through the resurrection of the dead, human beings will experience a gloriously transformed existence in 'the new heavens and the new earth' (2 Pet. 3: 13). Not only humanity but also the whole cosmos will be transfigured through and with the glory of Christ. In this ultimate union with Christ (John 14: 3), the earthly life of grace will pass over into the heavenly life of glory. The blessed will share in the ecstatic communion of mutual love that is the eternal life of the three divine persons.

Chapter 4
The sacraments and the Catholic Church

What rituals of worship and patterns of life shape the Catholic Church? Presenting the sacraments before dealing with the Church may seem like putting the cart before the horse. But the teaching of the Catholic Church did just that. Augustine and other fathers of the Church, some popes, some local councils, the Council of Florence (1438–45), and the Council of Trent (1545–63) taught much about baptism, the Eucharist, and the other sacraments long before official teaching on the nature and functions of the Church took shape at the First Vatican Council (1869/70) and, above all, at the Second Vatican Council (1962–5).

For those who wish to know more about the sacraments, the short answer would be attendance at the Easter Vigil on the evening of Holy Saturday. There the Rite for Christian Initiation of Adults (the RCIA), introduced in 1972 as a result of a mandate from Vatican II (*Sacrosanctum Concilium*, 64), reaches its climax and, after their long preparation, candidates are received into the Catholic Church through the sacraments of baptism, confirmation, and the Eucharist. The long answer is the first half of this chapter.

The seven sacraments

Unquestionably, the divine gifts are not limited to the seven sacraments of baptism, confirmation, Eucharist, penance, the anointing of the sick, holy orders, and matrimony. But they are seven central means for the common worship of God, privileged means that bring Catholics together in a community of mutual support and enable them to experience the risen Christ as effectively present in their lives. The sacraments are vivid, perceptible signs (that can be seen, heard, tasted, touched, and smelled); they create ritual dramas that take believers into a sacred time and place. They help participants to absorb the truths and values of Christian faith or allow such truths and values to revivify. They are a school of faith, a matrix for maturing faith. The sacraments confer and strengthen the new life of grace in the particular form that each sacrament symbolizes.

The word 'sacrament' in Latin originally referred to oath-taking, consecration, or ritual obligation. It came to mean some ritual action that blesses human beings with the saving life communicated through Christ's life, death, and resurrection and the outpouring of the Holy Spirit.

Christian initiation

I begin with baptism, confirmation, and the Eucharist. Together, these three sacraments constitute full initiation into Catholic life. These rites of initiation into the Church mark a movement away from one kind of identity and status to another. The initiated 'die' to a former way of life and are 'resurrected' or 'reborn' to another. From New Testament times, Christian initiation, or at least baptism, has been interpreted as a rite of death, burial, and resurrection (Rom. 6: 1–14) and rebirth (John 3: 5; Titus 3: 5). The stages of Christian initiation include *separation*, or entrance into the catechumenate; *preparation* or transition, when catechumens are instructed in Christian teaching and life and learn to pray with the community; and *celebration* (baptism, confirmation, and First Communion) by which the catechumens 'put on' Christ (Gal. 3: 26–7) and are incorporated into the one body of the community (1 Cor. 12: 13).

Baptism and confirmation

From the start of Christianity, the rite of baptismal washing and
initiation was understood to be one process of justification and
sanctification, in which the tripersonal God remits sins and
communicates new life, and in which human beings enter into the
Body of Christ (1 Cor. 6: 11). Like the dying and rising of Christ
himself, baptism has a once-and-for-all character; it can never be
repeated.

In controversies that flared up in the 4th and 5th centuries over
the worthiness or unworthiness of the one who administered
baptism, St Augustine of Hippo clarified for all time that the
validity and efficacy of the sacrament do not essentially depend
upon the personal holiness of the minister. The invisible Christ,
and not the visible minister, is the primary minister of baptism
and of the other sacraments. As Augustine put it, Christ is actively
present as the invisible minister of baptism, even if the sacrament
were to be visibly administered by an arch-traitor like Judas
Iscariot himself.

In the 14th and 15th centuries, the issue returned when John
Wyclif and John Huss argued that sacraments administered by a
sinful priest or bishop were not effective. In 1415, the Council of
Constance insisted that even 'a bad priest' truly and validly
administers the sacraments, provided he observes the essentials in
performing the sacraments and 'has the intention of doing what
the Church does'. The sinfulness of the minister (and/or the
sinfulness of the recipient) may stop baptism (and other
sacraments) from enjoying their full and fruitful effect. But it
would create an intolerable uncertainty about the validity (and
fruitfulness) of the sacrament if those receiving baptism or other
sacraments had to be sure that the minister was personally in a
state of grace and friendship with God. In his novel *The Power and
the Glory*, Graham Greene (1904–91) was a true Catholic follower
of Augustine: during a persecution in Mexico, people to whom a

sinful priest ministered knew they received the sacraments validly and fruitfully.

Eastern Catholics and other Eastern Christians have maintained the ancient practice of the Church: even in the case of infants, baptism, confirmation, and Holy Communion are administered together. But in the West, an anointing after baptism, associated with an imposition of hands and an invocation of the Holy Spirit, developed into a separate rite. This was administered by the bishop, who as head of the local church *confirmed* what had been done in baptism and incorporated the baptized fully into the community. Confirmation was to be delayed for years, with First Communion coming earlier at the age of reason. Postponed until adolescence or early adulthood, confirmation became the sacrament of a mature faith commitment. Any sense of the unified process of Christian initiation was widely lost.

Vatican II wanted to retrieve a richer sense of what confirmation brings: through this sacrament the faithful 'are more perfectly bound to the Church' and 'are, as true witnesses of Christ, more strictly obliged to spread the faith by word and deed' (*Lumen Gentium*, 11). Already given in baptism, the Holy Spirit descends more fully on those being confirmed and draws them into the witness that the Spirit gives to the Father and the Son (Rom. 8: 16–17).

The Eucharist

In an interconnected process of Christian initiation, baptism and confirmation reach their goal in the *Eucharist* (Greek for 'thanksgiving'). Unlike the other sacraments which were indirectly instituted by Christ, this sacrament comes directly from something that Jesus said and did at the end of his earthly life: the institution of the Eucharist during the Last Supper. Convergent New Testament traditions (from 1 Cor. 11: 23–6 and the Gospels) support this conclusion: at a sacrificial meal before he died, Jesus

8. The Last Supper and the figures of three prophets, a Greek miniature from the 5th or 6th century

invited his disciples to share, by eating and drinking, in his covenant offering to the Father. Elements of the Passover liturgy/meal were taken up and shaped the early Christian Eucharist, but it was very quickly celebrated every Sunday and not merely once a year (as in the case of the Jewish Passover). By the 3rd century, if not earlier, many Christians were celebrating the Eucharist on a daily basis.

In this sacrifice of praise, thanksgiving, and expiation for sins, Christ functioned as both priest and victim. His priestly words and gestures (the breaking of the bread/body and the 'pouring out of my blood') were clearly to be understood sacrificially. These words and actions symbolized and enacted a covenant of reconciliation that bound human beings in a new relationship with God and with one another. While the Last Supper formed a key element in his sacrifice, it was also a meal involving consecrated bread and wine: 'take and eat' and 'drink all of you' (Matt. 26: 26–7).

Out of its Jewish heritage, early Christianity developed a Liturgy of the Word to precede the Liturgy of the Eucharist. The former constitutes the first part of Mass, with opening prayers of praise and repentance, readings from the Bible (followed ideally by a homily), intercessions for the Church and the world, and (on important days) the Creed or confession of faith. Then follows the Liturgy of the Eucharist, with the preparation of the gifts, the *anamnesis*, *epiclesis*, and *doxology*, leading to the Lord's Prayer, a sign of reconciliation and peace, the reception of communion, and a final blessing. A single, integrated rite moves from word and worship to the Eucharistic meal. Several terms call for explanation.

The *anamnesis*, as remembering or recalling the past, involves bringing to mind the saving action of God in history, especially in the life, passion, death, resurrection, and glorification of Christ. As anticipation, *anamnesis* means looking forward to the time of final fulfilment and doing so with an expectation that already experiences something of that ultimate reality. Thus *anamnesis* entails memory, experience, and hope. St Paul incorporated these three elements into his account of the Eucharist: 'As often as you eat this bread and drink this cup, you proclaim [in the present] the death of the Lord [in the past] until he comes [in the future]' (1 Cor. 11: 26). The re-presentation here and now (in the shared eating, drinking, and 'proclaiming' of Christ's death and resurrection), the memorial of the foundational, once-and-for-all past event of salvation (the 'doing in remembrance' of Jesus who was handed over symbolically at the Last Supper and physically on Calvary), and the anticipation of his coming (which makes the Eucharist an anticipation of the final kingdom) are woven together in the liturgy. More than a thousand years later, the Pauline theme of Eucharistic experience, memory, and hope was expressed in a text for the feast of Corpus Christi (the feast of 'the Body of Christ' instituted in 1264 to celebrate the gift of the Eucharist):

> O sacred banquet in which Christ is received: the memory of his suffering is recalled [past], (our) mind is filled with grace [present], and we receive a pledge of the glory that is to be ours [future];
> (O sacrum convivium, in quo Christus sumitur, recolitur memoria passionis eius; mens impletur gratia; et futurae gloriae nobis pignus datur).

In the Eucharistic prayers the *epiclesis*, or 'invocation', normally asks that the Holy Spirit descend upon the gifts of bread and wine to change them into the body and blood of Christ for the transformation of those who receive them. In the new Eucharistic prayers introduced by the Catholic Church after Vatican II, the *epiclesis before* the narrative of the institution of the Eucharist prays that the Spirit may descend upon the gifts to transform them, while the *epiclesis after* the institution narrative prays that the communicants may be changed. Thus in *epiclesis* the Spirit is invoked and actualizes the Eucharistic presence of Christ; in *anamnesis* Christ is remembered, experienced, and anticipated. Then the *doxology*, or 'giving glory to God', completes the Eucharistic prayer, by directing 'all glory and honour' to God the Father, 'through, with, and in' Christ 'in the unity' created by the Holy Spirit.

Right from the beginning, Christians appreciated four particular blessings effected by the Eucharist: the *unity* of believers, who shared in Christ's perfect *sacrifice*, experienced his special *presence* through the consecrated elements, and were prepared for a glorious *resurrection*. First, Paul insisted that sharing in the one Eucharistic bread and in the one cup meant belonging to the one Body of Christ (1 Cor. 10: 16–17). A 5th-century prayer (from the *Liturgy of St Basil*) expressed this desire for Catholic unity: 'May all of us who partake of the one bread and chalice be united to one another in the communion of the same Holy Spirit.' Second, right from the time of the *Didache* (a text probably written about AD 90), Christians invoked Malachi 1: 11 to interpret the Eucharist as the 'pure sacrifice for the nations'. Third, they commonly appealed to the miracle at Cana (John 2: 1–11) and affirmed a profound change in the Eucharistic elements. Thus St Cyril of Jerusalem (d. 386) reminded his hearers: 'In Cana of Galilee he [Christ] changed water into wine (and wine is akin to blood). Is it incredible that he should change wine into blood? ... Therefore with complete assurance let us partake of these elements as being the body and blood of Christ' (*Mystagogic Catecheses*, 4. 2. 3). Fourth, St Irenaeus of Lyons (d. around 200) assured believers that by feeding 'on the flesh and blood of the Lord', their 'flesh' would enjoy the eternal life of resurrection (*Adversus Haereses*, 5. 2. 2–3).

In later centuries, two of these four blessings became controversial: first, the nature of the risen Christ's *presence* under the Eucharistic elements; and second, the *sacrificial character* of the Eucharist. From the 11th century, controversy emerged about the change in the Eucharistic elements and the nature of Christ's presence. A crudely realistic view of his presence and a purely symbolic version that excluded any real change in the elements marked the two extremes. Theologians and then official teaching began to apply 'transubstantiated' to what happens when the bread and wine become the body and blood of the risen Christ. The 'substance' of bread and wine are changed into Christ's body and blood, while the 'accidents', or secondary characteristics, of the elements remain. In the 16th century, Protestant Reformers raised again the issue of the Eucharistic presence. Some, like Ulrich Zwingli (1484–1531), maintained that the elements undergo no change whatsoever, and that the Lord's Supper is simply a memorial with only a 'spiritual' and merely symbolic meaning.

Faced with such challenges, the Council of Trent in a decree of 1551 affirmed the doctrine of 'transubstantiation', distinguished between the 'substance' and the 'outward appearances' (*species*) of bread and wine, but refrained from employing the pair of terms 'substance' and 'accidents', which through the influence of Thomas Aquinas had become normal usage. After acknowledging that 'we can hardly find words to express' Christ's presence in the Eucharist, Trent taught:

> by the consecration of the bread and wine there takes place a change in the whole substance of bread into the substance of the body of Christ our Lord and of the whole substance of wine into the substance of his blood. This change the holy Catholic Church has fittingly and properly named transubstantiation.

This was an attempt to find some middle ground between a purely symbolic and an ultra-realist view of the presence of Christ's body and blood in the Eucharist.

In its Constitution on the Sacred Liturgy of 1963, the Second Vatican Council did not use the term 'transubstantiation' and listed various ways through which Christ is vitally present in liturgical celebrations. This presence comes to its highpoint with the consecrated bread and wine upon the altar and his encounter with Christians in sacramental communion.

In the history of Christianity, the Eucharist as *sacrifice* became controversial much later than did the real presence of Christ in the Eucharist. St Cyprian of Carthage (d. 258) followed the Epistle to the Hebrews by calling Christ 'the high priest' who 'first offered himself as a sacrifice to the Father', and added that at the Eucharist 'the priest acts truly in Christ's stead ... and offers a true and complete sacrifice to God the Father' (*Epistola* 63, 14).

St John Chrysostom (d. 407) insisted that there is only one sacrifice. Just as there are not 'many Christs' but only one in every place, so there is only 'one sacrifice': 'we offer now what was offered then, an inexhaustible offering... We offer the same sacrifice or rather we make a memorial of that sacrifice' (*In Hebreos*, 3. 17). The human ministers ('we who offer') are secondary, visible ministers of the invisible Christ: 'He who did this at the supper is the same who now performs the act. We rank as ministers; it is he who consecrates and transmutes the elements' (*In Mattheum*, 82). The belief that the Eucharist is the sacramental 're-presentation' of the one, historical sacrifice of Christ and, as a sacrifice, involves ordained priests remained more or less unchallenged until the 16th century.

Many Protestant Reformers denied the sacrificial nature of the Eucharist and spoke of a meal which recalled the loving self-sacrifice of Christ. They feared that admitting the sacrificial value of the Eucharist would belittle his unique sacrifice. By denying the sacrificial nature of the Eucharist, such Reformers logically regarded ordination to the priesthood as superfluous: no sacrifice, and so no priests. The Council of Trent dedicated its 22nd session (1562) to the sacrifice of the Mass. It restated traditional Catholic teaching: the bloody sacrifice Christ offered once and for all 'on the altar of the cross' is 'offered' in 'an unbloody manner', but not repeated, 'under visible signs' to celebrate 'the memory' of Christ's 'passage from this world' and to apply 'the salutary power' of his sacrifice 'for the forgiveness of sins' and 'other necessities' of the faithful.

In the 20th century, many Catholics and other Christians, especially through dialogues with one another, came to realize that it is a false choice to speak of the Eucharistic liturgy as either a sacrifice or a memorial meal. It is the sacrificial meal of the new covenant. A renewed sense of the reality conveyed by the liturgical term *anamnesis* (remembrance) helped. The Eucharist as *anamnesis* makes effective in the present the past event of Christ's sacrifice. It 're-presents' the whole event of his life, death, resurrection, and sending of the Holy Spirit, bringing that unique past to be powerfully present now.

The 20th century also brought further developments in appreciating the Eucharist: for instance, as empowering work for justice and peace. It retrieved, above all, a sense of the Eucharist as the 'fountain from which flows all the power of the Church' and 'the summit towards which her activity is directed' (Vatican II, *Sacrosanctum Concilium*, 10). Being the supreme way of glorifying God and bringing about the sanctification of human beings, the Eucharist proves the greatest of the sacraments and the central act of worship in the life of the Church.

Penance and the anointing of the sick

After presenting the three sacraments that together constitute Christian initiation, I take up two sacraments available for sinful and sick Catholics.

Penance

The forgiveness of sins was a key feature in the ministry of Jesus. He imparted the divine pardon not only through his words (e.g. Luke 7: 47–50), but also through his action of establishing table fellowship with sinners and reconciling them with God. After his resurrection from the dead and the outpouring of the Holy Spirit, people entered the Church through baptism. What, then, was the situation of baptized Christians who committed sins and even reverted to the sinful lifestyle they had renounced at their baptism? In passing, the Gospels indicate procedures to be followed for the 'brother who does wrong' (Matt. 18: 15–18). Paul shows his anxious concern over sins committed by Christians in Corinth and prescribes remedies. For example, a man who is living in concubinage with his stepmother should be expelled from the community, 'so that his spirit may be saved on the day of the Lord' (1 Cor. 5: 5). The apostle also writes of someone who has suffered for his wrongdoing, but now should be forgiven and reconciled with the community (2 Cor. 2: 5–8).

Early Christians distinguished between lesser and death-dealing sins. Daily sins could be forgiven through prayer (in particular, the Lord's Prayer), fasting, works of mercy, and the Eucharist. Such death-dealing or serious sins as apostasy and adultery, however, called for a public process of reconciliation that could happen only once in a lifetime. Such sinners publicly acknowledged their sins (confession), and were kept apart from community worship for a period of penance, contrite prayer, and almsgiving (satisfaction). The penitents asked for prayers from other members of the community. When the bishop judged the repentance adequate, he restored the sinners to full communion through the imposition of hands (absolution). Thus the administration of penance, as it emerged in the 3rd century, was a *public* action of reconciliation that led to a lasting change of heart, involved the whole community, and was presided over by the bishop.

By the middle of the 5th century, however, this system had widely broken down – due to the vastly increased number of Christians, disruptions caused by the barbarian invasions, and other factors. The administration of penance was no longer totally public and limited to the ministry of bishops. Priests were delegated to be ministers of the sacrament, which now required strict secrecy.

The sacrament underwent an even more dramatic change from the end of the 6th century. Celtic and Anglo-Saxon monk-missionaries began fanning out across Europe, founding or re-founding Christian communities and introducing the 'monastic' practice of penance. This involved private confession to a spiritual father (or mother), an appropriate, even very severe penance (which aimed more at restoring the balance of the moral universe than at reconciliation with the community), and a private prayer of pardon and blessing after the penance (or satisfaction for sins) was completed. Besides making the sacrament of penance a private and non-liturgical matter, the monk-missionaries put an end to the situation of reconciliation for grave sins being available only once in a lifetime. The severity of the penances imposed meant, however, that fewer Christians practised sacramental penance.

In an attempt to correct this situation, the Fourth Lateran Council (1215) prescribed that the faithful should '*at least* once a year confess all their sins in secret to their own priest' and receive communion (italics mine). The spread of the Dominican, Franciscan, and other orders in the 13th century made the practice of confession more frequent in some Christian circles. But despite the desire of Lateran IV to increase sacramental practice, many limited themselves to confession and communion once a year.

In 1439, the Council of Florence spelled out more fully what the sacrament of 'penance' involved:

(1) 'contrition of heart which requires that one be sorry for the sin committed with the resolve not to sin in the future';

(2) 'oral confession which requires that sinners confess to their priests in their integrity all the [serious] sins they remember';

(3) 'the words of absolution spoken by the priest who has authority to absolve';

(4) 'satisfaction for the sin according to the judgement of the priest, which is mainly achieved by prayer, fasting, and almsgiving'.

In 1551, in response to the claim of some Reformers that sinners needed only interior conversion, the Council of Trent emphasized the importance of the sacrament of penance and specified further details in the scheme of contrition, confession, absolution, and satisfaction. It encouraged a sense that the sacramental rite of penance was an affair between God and a sinful individual. What many centuries of Catholics largely ignored was the relevance to the community of what they came to call 'confession'. They considered the sacrament a private event and a means of personal grace. They failed to recognize that the sins of the baptized harm the Church. The once-in-a-lifetime penitential discipline of early Christianity was obviously severe, but it did appreciate both the damage baptized Christians do to the whole body of Christ by their sins and the fact that repentance means being reconciled with the worshipping community and sharing again fully in its life.

The Second Vatican Council signalled a recovery of a communal perspective: 'Those who approach the sacrament of penance receive pardon from the mercy of God . . . and at the same time are reconciled with the Church which they have wounded by their sins' (*Lumen Gentium*, 11). This renewed sense that sacramental penance reconciles sinners with God *and with the Church* shows up vividly in the three rites for celebrating the sacrament found in the 'Order of Penance' promulgated by Pope Paul VI in 1973. He significantly introduced a new name, 'the sacrament of reconciliation'. But this sacrament, which actualizes and 're-presents' Christ's ministry to sinners, is still far from being fully used and appreciated by priests and people.

Anointing of the sick

The anointing of the sick is a sacrament closely associated with that of reconciliation and also draws on the example of Christ. He showed his love for the sick and sinful by healing them and forgiving their sins (e.g. Mark 2: 1–12). As a sacrament, the anointing of the sick took shape from the practice of Jesus and his first followers, and was inspired, in particular, by a passage from the Letter of James. The 'elders' had the specific role of 'praying over' the sick and anointing them with oil, understood to be endowed with special power from the Spirit. James invited the entire community to acknowledge to one another their sinfulness and pray for one another. They should expect the power of the risen Lord to be at work to save, raise, forgive, and heal the sick and sinful (Jas. 5: 14–16).

The sacrament came to be associated with the end of life and hence called 'extreme unction'. In 1439, the Council of Florence

9. On a visit to England in 1982, Pope John Paul II anoints and blesses the sick at Southwark Cathedral

reflected this shift: 'this sacrament may not be given except to a sick person whose life is feared for'. The minister of the sacrament is a priest, and 'its effect is the healing of the mind and (as far as it is good for the soul) of the body as well'. In the 16th century, the Council of Trent followed the teaching of Florence when insisting on the sacramental status of 'extreme unction' against the Reformers. The sacrament is 'to be administered to the sick, especially to those who are so seriously ill that they seem near to death; hence it is also called the sacrament of the dying'.

When restoring the original name of the sacrament, 'the anointing of the sick', Vatican II emphasized that 'it is not a sacrament only for those who are at the point of death'. It can and should be received by those suffering from serious illness and the onset of old age (*Sacrosanctum Concilium*, 73). Through the 1972 rite for the anointing of the sick, this sacrament has come to be celebrated much more frequently, and with a number of people often receiving it together in church. While maintaining the promise of saving and healing expressed by the Letter of James, the new rite invites the sick and the old to associate their suffering with the redeeming mission of Jesus for the good of the Church and the whole world.

Sacraments in the service of communion
Holy orders

To introduce holy orders, I refer readers to Chapter 1 and the section on 'early leadership', which traced the origins of authoritative ministry to the mission of Jesus and the organization of early churches. The first Christians, while enjoying the basic equality of all the baptized, were, nevertheless, led and served by some who performed specific ministries for them.

The letters of St Ignatius of Antioch (d. around 107) clarify the nature of Christian life in Asia Minor: a united community gathered around one bishop, who was assisted by presbyters and deacons. A 3rd-century document, the *Apostolic Tradition* of Hippolytus, describes the ordination (conferred by the imposition of hands and the invocation of the Holy Spirit) and ministry of bishops, presbyters, and deacons. Its guidelines for these holy orders remain thoroughly recognizable today in the Catholic Church, among the Orthodox, and beyond.

In the late Middle Ages, serious questions arose about the sacramental power of bishops and priests and came to a head in the 16th century. Protestant Reformers, who insisted (rightly) that all the baptized share a *common* priesthood, denied a *special* sacrament of holy orders that derived from Christ and the New Testament Church. Ministry, many of them argued, was a function delegated by Christian communities to some of their members, so as to ensure that the Word of God be preached well. In 1563, the Council of Trent, having upheld the sacrificial character of the Eucharist in its previous session (1562), insisted on the essential connection between sacrifice and priesthood and drew the conclusion: since 'the Catholic Church has received from the institution of Christ the holy, visible sacrifice of the Eucharist, it must also be acknowledged that there exists in the Church a new, visible, and external priesthood', which has 'the power of consecrating, offering, and administering his body and blood', as well as that of 'remitting sins'. The Council also maintained that bishops are 'superior' to priests, in as much as they 'govern the Church', 'ordain ministers', and 'confer the sacrament of confirmation'.

In a 1947 encyclical letter *Mediator Dei* ('the Mediator of God'), Pope Pius XII developed some teaching about holy orders that would prepare the way for the Second Vatican Council. All priesthood is founded in the one, unique priesthood of Christ, but the *ministerial* priesthood (conferred by the sacrament of holy orders) is to be distinguished from the *common* priesthood of all the faithful (conferred by baptism), and is exercised differently in the Eucharistic sacrifice, where priests 'represent the person of our Lord Jesus Christ' and 'act in the person of Christ'. At the same time, as the Pope stressed, all share in the one sacrifice of Christ, with the people offering the sacrifice 'through' and 'with' the priests.

At Vatican II, a fresh attention to Christ's triple role as prophet/herald, priest, and king/shepherd characterizes the Council's teaching on the common priesthood of the faithful, the ministry of bishops, and that of ordained priests. In particular, the prophetic, sanctifying, and pastoral role of presbyters means that their priesthood involves much more than merely fulfilling the cultic function exercised supremely in offering the sacrifice of the Eucharist.

Matrimony
Finally, what of the sacrament of matrimony? How did Christian marriage find its place among the seven sacraments?

Jesus drew images from weddings for some of his parables (e.g. Matt. 21: 1–14; 15: 1–13). John's Gospel reports how Jesus attended a wedding (John 2: 1–11); the other Gospels show how Jesus safeguarded the institution of marriage by excluding divorce and remarriage as contrary to God's will (Mark 10: 2–12). The Letter to the Ephesians appealed to the 'great mystery' of the union of all the baptized with Christ to encourage a startlingly elevated view of the loving relationship between husbands and wives. This powerful comparison implied the sacramental status of Christian marriage. Yet it took centuries for this implication to be fully elaborated.

From the 3rd century, Christians, while following the forms of marriage current in civil society, introduced some service of blessing and replaced the sacrificial rites of solemn Roman weddings with a celebration of the Eucharist. Moral teaching from the New Testament guided the way in which they lived out their married and family life. By the beginning of the second millennium, European rulers had turned over to bishops and their assistants the celebration of marriage and the administration of matrimonial matters. The liturgy for Christian marriage adopted many of the symbols used in civil ceremonies: for instance, the veil worn by the bride, her ring, and her joining hands with the bridegroom. The work of Thomas Aquinas and other medieval theologians clarified finally the sacramental status of Christian marriage. Hence in 1274 the Second Council of Lyons put marriage down on its list of seven sacraments.

Many of the Protestant Reformers, while maintaining the holiness of marriage, denied its sacramental status and rejected the juridical function of the Church in matrimonial matters. The Council of Trent in 1563 upheld the marriage of Christians as a sacrament instituted by Christ, whose 'grace perfects the natural love' of a married couple, 'confirms' their 'indissoluble union, and sanctifies' them. It insisted on the competence of the official Church in such matrimonial matters as the right and duty to determine the necessary conditions for contracting a valid

10. A Catholic wedding in a poor suburb of Nairobi, Kenya

marriage. The priest who blessed the marriage was understood to be an official witness and not the minister of the sacrament. Hence marriage stands apart from the other sacraments, in as much as those who 'minister' to each other are the bride and bridegroom.

The Second Vatican Council put married life within the context of the New Testament teaching that all the baptized are called to holiness – married people, no less than celibate priests and consecrated religious men and women (*Lumen Gentium*, 39–42). Vatican II went beyond Trent by calling marriage an 'intimate partnership of life and love' that involves 'total fidelity' and 'unbreakable unity' and by highlighting the importance of sexual love for the complete marriage relationship (*Gaudium et Spes*, 48–9).

The Catholic Church and her mission

Chapters 1 and 2 sketched the origin and history of the Catholic Church, its government, and such features as its being a community that embraces saints and sinners. The first part of this chapter has described the sacramental life of the Church. But, as I remarked above, official teaching about the nature and mission of the Church flowered late – only in the 19th and 20th centuries.

The heart of Jesus' preaching was the present and future Kingdom of God, which was, is, and will be forever a more encompassing reality than the Church. Nevertheless, from the 2nd century it was the institutional Church that drew attention and needed to be defended. Irenaeus called it 'the seven-branch candlestick which bears the light of Christ' (*Adversus Haereses*, 5. 20. 1). He thus referred to the origin of the Church in the Jewish people and implied the role of Jesus in founding this new assembly of God's people. Without proposing any detailed blueprint for the life and structures of the Church, Jesus had intended to build another Temple 'not made with hands' (Mark 14: 58; 15: 29), to introduce a universal covenant through his death and resurrection, and, by his choice of the Twelve headed by Peter, to reform the twelve tribes of Israel, and through them bring divine salvation to all the nations. Jesus was the Founder (upper case) of the Church, whereas the Twelve, Paul, and other apostles were the founders (lower case). In a wider sense, all Christians of the 1st century can be considered to have been in a variety of ways the founding fathers and founding mothers of the Church.

Irenaeus saw the Church as *one* by following 'one and the same way of salvation'; *holy* through 'the Spirit of God'; *catholic* in preaching 'the truth everywhere' and encompassing 'the whole world'; and *apostolic* by enjoying the 'true and solid' tradition coming through the bishops from the apostles (*Adversus Haereses*, 3. 24; 5. 20). The 4th-century Nicene-Constantinopolitan Creed would enshrine unity, holiness, catholicity, and apostolicity as the four 'marks', or essential characteristics, of the Church. But we find them already endorsed 200 years earlier by Irenaeus. He insisted perhaps most of all on 'apostolicity', stressing a lasting fidelity to the foundations of Christian faith taught by Peter, Paul, and the other apostles. If he lived today, Irenaeus would be glad to see this fidelity symbolized by the massive statues of Peter and Paul that flank St Peter's Square in Rome.

From the early 5th-century, barbarian invasions from the North ravaged Europe and parts of North Africa. From the early 7th century, Muslim forces began to take over much of the Middle East; by the early 8th century, Islam had taken possession of North Africa and Spain. In those turbulent times, the spiritual and, to some extent, the political authority of the Bishop of Rome developed. The primacy of Peter and his successors was supported by appeals to the language of Matthew 16: 18–19 about the founding of the Church on the rock of Peter and his being given the keys of the Kingdom. At the Council of Chalcedon in 451, after the bishops had listened to the Letter to Flavian written by Pope Leo I, they exclaimed: 'Peter has spoken through the mouth of Leo.'

From the 6th century, the title of 'patriarch' was given to the bishops of Rome, Constantinople, Alexandria, Antioch, and Jerusalem. The patriarchs exercised wide authority in such matters as appointing bishops of major dioceses and judging appeals to their jurisdiction. For Leo the Great, Gregory the Great (pope 590–604), and other leading popes in the first millennium, the Bishop of Rome was meant to be the centre of unity in the true faith and the last court of appeal in matters involving the 'Catholic faith that comes to us from the apostles' (Roman Canon or First Eucharistic Prayer). As we saw in Chapter 1, various forces conspired to bring a tragic break, traditionally dated to the mutual excommunications of July 1054, between the Patriarch of Constantinople, or Ecumenical Patriarch, and the Bishop of Rome, or Patriarch of the West.

The centralizing policies of Gregory VII (pope 1073–85) and Innocent III (pope 1198–1216) involved papal claims to exercise jurisdiction over the whole Church and even to dictate to temporal rulers in such major secular matters as the election of the Holy

Roman Emperor. The armies of popes were involved in wars – right down to the unification of Italy in 1870. Thanks to John XXIII, John Paul II, and other modern popes, the complete military irrelevance of the papacy has coincided with its greatest moral authority. In a world that continues to be ravaged by savage nationalism and war, the loss of the papal states in 1870 has led to the pope becoming the incumbent of the world's most prominent and influential religious office. Over 170 nations have entered diplomatic relations with the tiny Vatican State; presidents, prime ministers, and other political leaders arrive regularly for meetings with the pope.

All of this has happened despite Christendom being divided, first by the 11th-century break with the Orthodox, and then in the 16th century. The Protestant Reformers, headed by Martin Luther, rejected papal authority in their campaign to bring the Church into line with New Testament faith, but did not (at least initially) envisage a divided Christendom. Although it was called to clarify teaching and reform abuses, the Council of Trent dealt with other issues (see Chapter 2) and not directly with questions of the Church and the papacy.

In a world shaken by the French Revolution and social unrest, many rulers continued to promote the independence of national churches at the expense of wider Christian unity. Catholics looked for a stronger papacy to check abuses and save Christianity from lapsing into religious indifference. At the First Vatican Council (1869–70), the bishops solemnly approved two pieces of teaching about the papal office: firstly, a primacy of jurisdiction over the whole Church; and secondly, papal infallibility.

Primacy was understood to confer a universal authority that allowed the pope to intervene anywhere, without depending on the permission of the local bishop. The Council added, however, that this papal primacy was intended to support and not belittle the God-given authority of the bishops in their dioceses.

Infallibility concerned a possibility for the teaching office of the pope that has rarely been exercised: for instance, in the 1950 solemn definition by Pius XII of the assumption of the Blessed Virgin Mary – namely, that at the end of her earthly life she was taken up, body and soul, into heavenly glory. An infallible teaching is one that invokes the fullness of papal authority (*ex cathedra*) as universal pastor and successor of St Peter, and concerns some revealed truth that all Christians should believe. Hence such papal infallibility is not involved when the pope teaches on matters other than revealed faith and morals. Nor can infallibility be recognized when it is not manifestly clear that the pope wants to teach *ex cathedra*. Thus the 1968 encyclical on married life and love, *Humanae Vitae* ('Of human life'), which rejected the use of artificial means of birth control, cannot be considered an exercise of the infallible teaching office. Paul VI never claimed that, nor did he use the language which would warrant it being considered *ex cathedra* teaching.

By concentrating on papal primacy and infallibility, Vatican I left much to be completed. In its Constitution on the Church (*Lumen Gentium*) and other documents, Vatican II filled out some teaching on the nature and function of the Church in herself and in her relations with others. At least five points should be retrieved.

(1) For many centuries, a sharp distinction prevailed between clergy and laity, as if there were two classes of Christians. Even today, many people ignore the fact that all the baptized make up the Church, and speak of 'the Church' when they mean only the bishops and priests. Vatican II insisted that *all* the baptized constitute the People of God and are equally called to holiness and to participate in the mission of the Church.

(2) A generous variety of images (e.g. the Body of Christ, People of God, and Temple of the Holy Spirit) witnesses to the rich reality of the Church. No single description can by itself express adequately all that the Church is and should be.

(3) The reign of God, despite recurrent challenges and setbacks, is steadily growing to its final completion. The Church exists for this Kingdom, and is to be understood in its light, and not vice versa.

(4) The Church is simultaneously holy and sinful, and must constantly 'follow the path of penitence and renewal' (*Lumen Gentium*, 8).

(5) The teaching role and responsibility for the whole Church belongs to the entire college of bishops through their episcopal ordination and being in communion with the bishop of Rome. While this 'collegiality' is a new term, it finds its source in the original college of apostles led by St Peter.

Finally, Vatican II launched a new era in the Catholic Church's relations with other Christian communities, with Jews, and with the followers of different world religions. Dialogue with and outreach to all these 'others' has already produced much fruit. But the healing of so many divisions in the Christian and human family still remains a matter of prayerful hope and generous commitment.

Chapter 5
Catholic moral life and teaching

Previous chapters have recalled the dignity of all human beings, created in the divine image and likeness, enabled by Christ's grace and the power of the Spirit to share in the life of God, and called to eternal glory beyond death (Chapter 3). Catholics (and other Christians) are consecrated and nourished by the sacraments and by their communion in the Church's life and worship (Chapter 4). How then should they behave? What principles should guide their moral life and decision-making? How might the holiness with which they have been blessed express itself in their daily existence?

At its best, Catholic teaching on the moral life is noble and convincing, as in a summary statement from John Paul II's 1993 encyclical *Veritatis Splendor* ('The splendour of truth'): 'Jesus' way of acting and his words – his deeds and his precepts – constitute the moral rule of Christian life.' At its worst, some teachers have deformed that teaching. The liberal views of Antonino Diana (1586–1663), for instance, could accommodate various forms of human violence and robbery. That led him to be nicknamed 'the lamb of God', since in his own way he could 'take away the sins of the world'. He has his latterday successors: for example, in such Catholic thinkers who 'generously' extend just-war theory to tolerate and even recommend pre-emptive strikes.

Historical developments

Jesus and the authors of the New Testament maintained much of the moral teaching that they had inherited from the Old Testament. Jesus innovated by putting together in one love-command the hitherto distinct commandments to love God (Deut. 6: 5) and to love one's neighbour (Lev. 19: 18), by teaching a love for one's enemies (Matt. 5: 43–8), and by practising an equality that was shockingly new in that women belonged to the travelling band of his disciples (Luke 8: 1–3). But, in general, Jesus, Paul, and other early Christians endorsed what Judaism had taught about right and wrong behaviour, above all through the Ten Commandments. Jesus and his first followers, however, never endorsed armed violence, as did some texts in the Hebrew Bible.

The *Didache* shows that a lengthy catechesis on moral matters, as well as on doctrines of Christian faith, had emerged by the end of the 1st century. Both the *Didache* and the roughly contemporary *Epistle of Barnabas* developed a moral teaching that contrasted 'the way of life' with 'the way of death'. Their respect for life included rejecting abortion and infanticide, both of which were widely practised by non-Christians.

A straight line leads from this very early teaching to the Second Vatican Council, which described abortion and infanticide as 'abominable crimes' (*Gaudium et Spes*, 51), and to John Paul II's *Evangelium Vitae* ('The gospel of life'). His concern for life entailed rejecting abortion as 'a grave moral disorder' and a decision 'against the weakest and most defenceless of human beings' (nos. 28, 62, 70). He repudiated a 'culture of death', which countenances euthanasia (in such forms as physician-assisted suicide) and killing or deliberately shortening the life of handicapped infants.

Evangelium Vitae also pleaded for life in two further ways. It called 'the use of human embryos or foetuses' for experiments 'a crime against their dignity as human beings who have a right to the same respect owed to a child once born' (no. 63). It excluded the death penalty, 'except in the case of absolute necessity', or 'when it would not be possible otherwise to defend society'. The pope added: 'today, however, as a result of steady improvements in the organization of the penal system, such cases are very rare, if not practically non-existent' (no. 56).

In the centuries that followed the *Didache*, Christian leaders continued to address moral issues. St Augustine of Hippo (d. 430), for instance, gave the highest importance to truth-telling and condemned lying as something that could not be justified by allegedly good intentions. He deserves to be heard in a world where truth, at best, has often become a fairly trifling affair and, at worst, is systematically distorted and perverted. Some teachers, like Pope Gregory the Great (d. 604), spelled out the seven deadly sins, or sins traditionally considered to be the root of all other sins and the major threat to a genuinely moral life: pride, avarice or covetousness, lust, envy, gluttony, anger, and sloth. In the Middle Ages, St Thomas Aquinas (d. 1274) developed thinking about the 'natural law', constituted by those universally valid moral principles which are discoverable by human reason and should govern social institutions and personal morality. A little later, Dante (d. 1321) brought together doctrine and a detailed account of the moral life. His *Divine Comedy* remains a vivid handbook for the practical life of Christians. He constructed the long climb up the mountain of purgatory around seven terraces on which sinners are cleansed of the seven deadly sins, which began with the worst (pride) and ended with the least serious sin of lust. Through both the *Purgatorio* and the *Inferno*, Dante showed how evil acts deform people.

It was not, however, until modern times that theologians and official teachers of the Church began developing a distinct body of moral teaching. For centuries they had endorsed a single, broadly agreed version of virtue and the virtuous life. This largely unchallenged moral consensus tolerated, however, the use of torture and the institution of slavery. In the case of criminals, suspected heretics, and others, popes and theologians, almost without exception, accepted the use of torture to maintain the religious and social stability of their society. A firm rejection of any 'physical and mental torture' finally came in the Second Vatican Council's teaching on respect for the human person (*Gaudium et Spes*, 27). Notoriously, many governments, so long as they can escape too much adverse criticism, still practise or allow torture to be practised by their security forces and, if necessary, 'outsource' such 'advanced interrogation techniques' to less squeamish (and less publicly accountable) countries.

Their Jewish heritage and the widespread presence of slaves in Graeco-Roman society did nothing to encourage the first Christians to question the institution of slavery, even if they certainly moderated its worst features. Some New Testament letters contained rules of conduct for Christian slave-owners as well as slaves: 'Masters, treat your slaves justly and fairly, for you know that you also have a Master in heaven' (Col. 4: 1). Across Christian Europe, slavery was gradually transformed into the much milder system of serfdom. Sadly, the discovery of America by Columbus in 1492 initiated a new period of slave-traffic and slave-owning. Pope Paul III in 1537 and other popes condemned the slave trade. But many Catholics (and other Christians) continued to consider slavery compatible with the natural law and justifiable under certain circumstances. In the name of the essential equality of all human beings, Vatican II denounced 'any kind of slavery, whether social or political' (*Gaudium et Spes*, 29). In his encyclical *Veritatis Splendor*, John Paul II called slavery 'intrinsically evil' (no. 80). In retrospect, one can see how Catholics continued to draw their moral standards about slavery at least in part from existing social patterns. They failed for centuries to see what was demanded by Christ's love-command and by their belief that all human beings have been created in the divine image and likeness.

One can add further examples of striking developments in Catholic moral doctrine: firstly, the teaching on social justice developed by Pope Leo XIII and his successors; secondly, the teaching on universal human rights (and their correlative duties) set out in John XXIII's 1963 encyclical *Pacem in Terris* ('Peace on earth') and vigorously elaborated by John Paul II; and thirdly, the sensitivity (which emerged after Vatican II) to ecological issues and the retrieval from St Francis of Assisi (d. 1226) of a loving view of nature that excludes the dreadful and dangerous abuse of the earth and its resources. Our planet cannot continue to be a life-giving environment unless human beings quickly become much more responsible stewards of the created world.

Such developments of Catholic moral thinking and teaching have come slowly, sometimes with shameful slowness. Yet they illustrate a willingness to learn, through experience and a prayerful discernment, what the divine love revealed in Jesus Christ demands of his followers. The results of those developments reached a provisional highpoint with Vatican II's 1965 Pastoral Constitution on the Church in the Modern World. This was the first far-reaching and fairly complete Catholic document on the moral life to come from a council or a pope.

Distinctive moral convictions

In the light of historical developments, it seems illuminating to track several moral convictions rooted in Catholic thinking and behaviour. I am not alleging that these convictions are unique to Catholicism, but only that they are distinctive and persistent.

Respect for life

Vatican II and John Paul II, as we have seen above, showed a deep concern to elaborate a consistent ethic in support of human dignity and life. The Constitution on the Church in the Modern World devoted a whole chapter to the fostering of peace and establishing an effective community of nations (nos. 77–90). The

Catholicism

11. John Paul II meeting the Dalai Lama, who joined the Pope for the inter-faith 'Day of Prayer for Peace' at Assisi in 1986

Council, in the face of new weapons that 'can inflict immense and indiscriminate havoc', called for 'a completely fresh appraisal of war', and endorsed condemnations of 'total war' (which had already come from Pius XII, John XXIII, and Paul VI). The Council also condemned as 'frightful crimes' the 'extermination' of entire races, nations, or ethnic minorities (ibid. 79–80). In particular, it had in mind here the six million Jewish victims of Nazi genocide, an unspeakable crime against God and humanity that John Paul II made a repeated theme of speeches and sermons from the start of his pontificate.

Gaudium et Spes, along with a deep concern to 'curb the savagery of war', nevertheless acknowledged that 'as long as the danger of war persists and there is no international authority with the necessary competence and power, governments cannot be denied the right of lawful self-defence, *once all peace efforts have failed*' (ibid. 79; italics mine). This was tantamount to accepting the possibility of a just defence (to be distinguished from holy wars, crusades, and pre-emptive strikes). But in some tragic recent

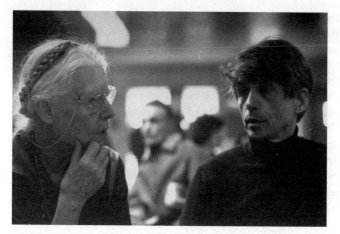

12. Dorothy Day, an American peace campaigner and social activist, meeting her younger counterpart, Father Daniel Berrigan, S.J.

examples, war has been declared not only before exhausting all efforts at peace but also in the cause of national self-aggrandizement.

Respect for human life characterizes the Catholic tradition (or at least the best features of the Catholic tradition) – right from the early teaching in support of 'the way of life' provided by the *Didache* and the *Epistle of Barnabas*. One can track a trajectory down to Pope Benedict XVI that shows respect for life to be a distinctive (but not unique) characteristic of Catholic morality.

The sexual order

Men and women were both created in the image and likeness of God and, in general, can find through marriage their human and religious fulfilment (Chapters 3 and 4 above). From the start of Christianity, respect for the personal and social values of human sexuality and a desire to nourish healthy family life underpinned a teaching that defended a middle ground between two extremes: a widespread licentiousness and shameful treatment of women, on the one hand, and the belittling of the goodness of married people's sexual life that came from such groups as the Manicheans and the Cathars, on the other.

In the immediate post-New Testament period, we find the *Didache* and the *Epistle of Barnabas* warning against 'the way of darkness' by repudiating three kinds of sexual activity that the Catholic tradition would consistently repudiate – premarital sex, extramarital sex, and homosexual practices: 'You shall not commit fornication; you shall not commit adultery; you shall not engage in homosexual activity' (*Epistle of Barnabas*, 19. 4; *Didache*, 2. 2). In all three cases, down through the ages many people, including not a few Catholics and other Christians, have dissented from this teaching. But in doing so, they have been overriding the clear judgement of the New Testament scriptures and the mainstream tradition. But what of sexuality and Catholic married life?

From the time of Pius XI's encyclical letter *Casti Connubii* ('Of chaste marriage'), Catholic teaching has taken up the challenge of holding together the two obvious purposes of marital intercourse: the fostering of mutual love and the begetting of children. Clearly tensions will arise between these two purposes. Responsible parenthood must reckon with such factors as the lack of proper housing for a larger family, the precarious health of one or other of the spouses, economic difficulties, and the dramatic growth in the world's population. Pius XI recognized the legitimacy of natural family planning (or choosing the safe or sterile period for intercourse), but rejected medical contraception as morally wrong.

Vatican II couched its teaching in general terms, encouraging in spouses 'a sense of human and Christian responsibility'. With 'docile reverence towards God' and 'common counsel and effort', they should reach 'a right judgement' about having further children (*Gaudium et Spes*, 50–1). Methods of birth control were discussed not by the Council but by a commission of experts. In 1966, they presented a final report to Pope Paul VI; a strong majority on the commission recommended a change in the teaching coming from Pius XI. Paul VI did not, however, follow the advice of the majority. In his 1968 encyclical *Humanae Vitae* ('Of human life'), while recognizing the importance of married love and endorsing responsible parenthood, he rejected contraception. He appealed to the inseparable connection between the unitive and procreative meaning of sexual intercourse, and declared that 'each and every marriage act' must be open to the transmission of life (no. 11). While being an authoritative statement, the encyclical was not an infallible document (see Chapter 4 above). The bishops of many countries, including Cardinal Albino Luciani of Venice (to become Pope John Paul I in 1978), introduced mitigating nuances into the papal teaching and would not unconditionally exclude artificial means of birth control.

In his papal teaching, John Paul II, while saying nothing about any means adopted, repeatedly condemned contraception as gravely wrong. He also firmly distinguished contraception from abortion as '*specifically different* evils'. Unlike contraception, abortion 'directly violates the divine commandment: "You shall not kill"' (*Evangelium Vitae*, 13; italics his).

Around the world, innumerable Catholic couples, after prayer and reflection, have conscientiously reached their own conclusion on what responsible parenthood requires of them. Here they can be encouraged by the words of Vatican II: 'it is the spouses themselves who must ultimately make this judgement' (*Gaudium et Spes*, 50).

Justice and charity

The Christian tradition has called justice a *cardinal* ('hinge') virtue, because right human conduct pivots upon it. Thomas Aquinas described justice as 'the strong and firm will to give each his due'. From the time of Leo XIII's encyclical *Rerum Novarum* of 1891 and its insistence of what justice demands for 'the interests of the poorer populations', social justice became a key theme in

Catholic teaching. It aims to remove whatever excludes groups and individuals from participating in society and even condemns them to living on the margins of society. A synod of bishops meeting in Rome in 1971 summed up its commitment to social justice: 'Action on behalf of justice and participation in the transformation of the world' are 'a constitutive dimension of the preaching of the Gospel, or, in other words, of the Church's mission for the redemption of the human race and its liberation from every oppressive situation'.

Love, even more than considerations of justice, has inspired Catholics and other Christians to care for any man or woman in need. Christianity inherited from the Old Testament a healthy message of concern for widows, orphans, and strangers, along with prophetic opposition to those who used their wealth and power to oppress the economically and socially weak. Jesus expected his followers to help the hungry, the thirsty, strangers, the naked, the sick, and prisoners (Matt. 25: 31–46). His parable of the Good Samaritan called for a willingness to reach across religious and cultural divides to assist any human being in distress (Luke 10: 30–7). These passages in Matthew 25 and Luke 10, along with the parable of the rich man and the poor Lazarus (Luke 16:19–31), have inspired Catholics and other Christians for 2,000 years.

The words of Jesus have stimulated innumerable Catholics to staff hospitals – not least, women who belong to religious institutes founded specifically to care for the sick, the housebound, and the terminally ill. A parallel and equally generous commitment by lay and religious Catholics to the work of educating children, young people, and adults has been fired by the sense of Jesus saying to them: 'I was ignorant and you taught me.'

Forming our conscience

John Paul II called conscience 'the proximate norm of personal morality' (*Veritatis Splendor*, 60). This statement cohered with a long Catholic tradition and with the teaching of Vatican II: 'In the

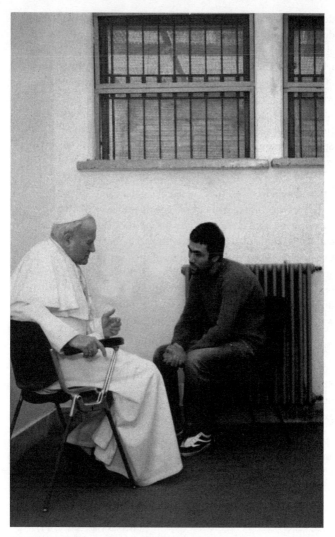

13. John Paul II in a prison cell visiting Mehmet Ali Agca, who tried to assassinate the Pope on 13 May 1981

depths of their conscience human beings detect a law which they do not make for themselves but which they must obey. Its voice always summons them to love and to do what is good and to shun what is evil.' The Council also realistically recognized the attitude of all those who 'take little care to seek what is true and good' and whose conscience 'through a habit of sin' gradually becomes 'almost blind' (*Gaudium et Spes*, 16). Paul states the remedy. Our sinful minds need to be transformed and renewed by the Holy Spirit before we can 'discern the will of God' and know 'what is good, acceptable, and perfect' (Rom. 12: 2).

There should be no escape from applying the moral law to the concrete circumstances of life and conscientiously deciding on what is to be done (*Veritatis Splendor*, 54–64). This is far from endorsing a kind of facile self-determination that claims the right to determine for oneself 'the criteria of good and evil and then acts accordingly' (ibid. 32). For Catholics and other Christians, forming one's conscience means attending with utter seriousness to the divine law and letting it shape one's heart, mind, and life. Jesus wanted nothing less from his followers (Mark 7: 20–3).

Following one's conscience converges with following Christ and taking to heart his loving, generously self-forgetful style of life. St Paul pointed to Christ as the supreme moral exemplar. St Irenaeus, among the most Pauline of the Church fathers, expressed beautifully what such discipleship entails:

> There is no other way for us to learn than to see our Teacher and hear his voice with our own ears. It is by becoming imitators of his actions and doers of his words that we have communion with him. It is from him who has been perfect from before all creation that we, so lately made, receive fulfilment.
>
> (Adversus Haereses, 5. 1. 1)

Chapter 6
Characteristics of Catholicism

Any interested observer can see how Catholicism varies considerably around the world. To sense the diversity it would be enough to start from Catania (Sicily) and its exuberant observance of the feast of St Agatha (5 February), visit Kerala (South India) and attend Mass in a Syro-Malabar church, and travel further to the highlands of Papua New Guinea and share in a Sunday Eucharist celebrated in pidgin. The culturally, geographically, and ritually diverse character of Catholic worship and life raises the question: What holds it all together? Which authentically Catholic instincts and concerns shape and unify the world's oldest and largest institution that has spread almost everywhere? Is there such a thing as an identifiable Catholic worldview, and are there characteristics of Catholicism that show through the variety of cultural and ritual expressions of Catholic life around the globe?

One might point to governance by bishops (assisted by priests and deacons) who, by leading their dioceses and remaining in communion with the Bishop of Rome, keep the Catholic Church together. Or one could go deeper and name the celebration of the seven sacraments and, above all, the Eucharist ('the sacrament of sacraments', Thomas Aquinas) as the force that identifies and unites Catholics everywhere. There is a special Catholic emphasis on attending the Sunday Eucharist, and there is a particular

Catholic intensity about receiving Christ in Holy Communion and praying before his presence in the Blessed Sacrament. One can feel very close to the heart of Catholicism at a parish Mass on Sundays, especially in the moments after Holy Communion. Among Catholics everywhere, the Eucharist focuses commitment to Christ and acts as a powerful collective force. In modern Ireland and around the world, many teachers used to quote the summary of Irish faith and practice offered by Augustine Birrell (Chief Secretary for Ireland from 1908 to 1916) in a report that he sent to London: 'it is the Mass that matters'.

But can we dive deeper than particular religious rituals, beliefs, and practices that bring Catholics together and hold them together? What characteristics pervade their worship, belief, and practice? We can name three such characteristics: a desire to incorporate all material reality into their sacramental and devotional life, a willingness to practise the principle of 'both/and', and a deep concern for unity.

The material world and God's grace

At the birth of Christianity, St Paul's Letter to the Romans bears witness to the conviction that the transforming light of the good news and the power of baptism (and the other sacraments) must be brought to bear on a sinful world. Before the reading or singing of the Gospel, Catholics make the sign of the cross on their foreheads, mouth, and breast. That is a vivid way of declaring that the message of the crucified Christ should heal and transform their thoughts, words, and affections. At the same time, the sacraments themselves witness to the God-oriented character of all created reality, an orientation that has been radically enhanced by the incarnation. Through being ennobled by the incarnation, the material world has become even more the theatre of divine grace and mediates God's blessings. The ordinary, everyday things of life mediate the divine presence and invite a human response.

Catholic Christianity has fostered the sense that all human reality and, indeed, the whole material cosmos have been touched, blessed, and changed by the 'Word becoming flesh' (John 1: 14). From the 2nd century AD, Gnostics have repeatedly taken redemption to mean the human spirit escaping from the body and from an evil, material world. Against such aberrations, St Irenaeus refused to downplay matter. He insisted on the goodness of the created world in general and of the human body in particular. An essential dignity has been conferred on our bodies not only through their origin (in God's creation) and their destiny (in the resurrection to come) but also (and even more) through the incarnation of the Son of God. By assuming 'flesh' (the complete human condition of body and spirit), the Son of God ratified the inherent value of men and women created in God's image and likeness (Gen. 1: 26–7). When they are baptized into Christ and receive him in the Eucharist, their intimate contact with him will bring them to their own resurrection and union with the glorious Body of Christ in the life to come.

One can trace a clear trajectory from Irenaeus' championing of the 'enfleshment' of God's Son and the dignity of bodily humanity down through the centuries, not least down to Christmas cribs in Italy and elsewhere and to Italian artists portraying the child Jesus at Mary's breast – both forceful ways of bringing out the true (bodily and spiritual) humanity of the incarnate Word of God. The incarnation of the Son of God, together with the life, death, resurrection, and sending of the Holy Spirit that followed, transformed the physical reality of the created world.

Material realities, such as water, bread, wine, oil, and human bodies, have now been lifted to a new level and spiritualized, so as to become the channels of God's self-revelation and bearers of the divine holiness. Through the seven sacraments of the Church, things that we can see, hear, touch, taste, and smell impart the divine truth and power. The water poured in baptism, bread and wine consecrated at the Eucharist, hands imposed in ordination, oil smeared on the foreheads and hands of the sick, bodies joined in matrimony, and other perceptible signs that constitute the sacraments communicate various spiritual blessings and a share in the life of the tripersonal God. The sacraments of the Catholic Church transfigure the material elements and actions of a world that is already 'charged with the grandeur of God' (Gerard Manley Hopkins, 'God's Grandeur').

The sacramentalizing of the material world and of human life finds its heart in the seven sacraments that initiate and nourish a share in the life of the all-holy God. But this spiritualizing of the world and human beings extends beyond the seven sacraments: in particular, to such sacramentals (material things that become sacred signs) as the ashes Catholics receive on their foreheads on Ash Wednesday and the palms they carry home on Palm Sunday. In the proper sense, sacramentals are holy practices, prayers, and all manner of popular devotions and objects officially approved and blessed in the Catholic Church. They include some of the traditions that were fostered by Franciscans and Dominicans and have never lost their popularity: for example, making the Stations of the Cross (especially during the weeks leading up to Good Friday), Christmas cribs, which recall Christ's birth among us, and the saying of the rosary. In Chapter 1, we mentioned these and other practices, which consecrate to God through Christ the whole of life. That chapter also cited the much older practice of pilgrimages, which can bring a fresh start in life and inculcate a sense of human existence as one long spiritual journey.

Together with pilgrimages, structures (catacombs, churches, and monasteries) and religious art played their part in sacralizing life right from the early centuries of Catholic Christianity. Obviously, buildings and visual images have remained central to the performance of official worship. But even when the sacraments are not being administered, churches, paintings, statues, mosaics, altarpieces, and stained-glass windows are there to lift to God the minds and hearts of those who visit. For Eastern Christians, both

Orthodox and Catholics, icons are endued with divine power and help the whole world to symbolize God. Almost as old as Christian art, 'holy water', or water that has been blessed, has been used for such spiritual purposes as cleansing and dedication from at least the 4th century.

Some of the very old sacramentals, such as the palms distributed on Palm Sunday, derive from the history of Jesus – in this case, from his entrance into Jerusalem shortly before he died (Mark 11: 8). Other sacramentals, such as the usage of sweet-smelling incense, go back even further, in this case to rites practised in the Jerusalem Temple (Ps. 141: 2). The scented smoke of burning incense that rose to God meant 'squandering' something costly in a gift of unreserved love. Incense has maintained a central place in the worship of Orthodox Christians. Catholics use it frequently: in processions, at the celebration of Mass, and for funeral rites.

Living for more than 30 years in Italy, I enjoyed customs associated with religious feasts. During the Christmas season, we ate *panettone*, a bread made with eggs, dried fruit, and butter. Easter brought the *colomba*, or dove-shaped cake. In other countries, hot-cross buns, or buns marked with a cross, are available on Good Friday. In Spain, Italy, and some Spanish-speaking countries, people eat sweets called 'the bones of the saints' when All Saints' Day and All Souls' Day come around on 1 and 2 November, respectively. Such customs link the secular (in this case, eating) with the sacred, and punctuate the year in a way that gently reinforces a sense of moving through holy time to a final meeting with God.

Saints and their earthly stories also play a part in spiritualizing the year and the movement of human life, as well as in supporting a sense of national identity. It can be a matter of celebrating annually the feast day of a saint who has a special connection with some nation, city, village, parish, shrine, or person. On 17 March,

Irish Catholics around the world continue to celebrate with gusto the feast of St Patrick; Scots and those of Scottish origin do the same on 30 November, the feast of St Andrew, their patron saint. On 13 June, Italians pack into Padua for the feast of St Antony (d. 1231), a Franciscan friar who spent the last years of his life in or near that city. Many Catholics, year by year, observe their 'name day', the feast day of the saint after whom they are called. Although the day of their birth may not coincide with the feast day of their saint, it is the feast day that often counts for more with them and their families. Sometimes the special 'function' of a saint figures prominently on the feast day. Thus St Antony (d. 356), an Egyptian Christian who organized the life of hermits in the desert, is celebrated in Italy and elsewhere as a friend and protector of animals – and, by extension, of goldfish, canaries, and other pets. On his feast day, 17 January, the Mass ends with wine and sweet bread being distributed to the faithful as they leave the church, while an assortment of animals receives a blessing outside (and sometimes inside). At St Eusebius in Rome, this event has become so popular that the cats, dogs, and horses, which used to be able to fit into the church, now have to wait in the square to be blessed with their owners.

Around the world, Catholics use a wide variety of blessings for their homes, their workplaces, and other material things that enter their lives and should be consecrated to become part of joining Christ in a pilgrimage home to God. Thus there are blessings for factories, farms, homes, hospitals, libraries, offices, shops, aircraft, motor cars, and ships (including fishing fleets). Blessings are available for engaged couples, families, nurses and doctors (with their patients), teachers (along with students at the beginning of the academic year), travellers, and further categories of persons. The urbanizing of the world and the flight from the land may have meant, for a while, a decline in such practices. But now blessings seem to be booming again, and many families treasure, for example, the annual blessing of their homes at Easter-tide. Through such sacramentals, the powerful presence of

Christ in every aspect of bodily and human existence can become more perceptible.

Some people fear that such practices can lapse into magical superstition. But this will not happen so long as believers remember firstly that blessings and other sacramentals aim at putting all times, places, and activities into a relationship with Christ, and secondly, that living together their faith in Christ as truly divine and fully human is the heart of the matter (and not some less important devotions).

Catholics know how daily life can be spiritualized and 'sacramentalized' through the statues of Jesus or his saints in their sitting-room or kitchen and images on the walls of their bedrooms and elsewhere in their homes. For Christians everywhere, the family forms the utterly essential group within society. The future of the world and the Church depends on this sacred unit. Many Catholic (and other Christian) families draw inspiration from Christmas cribs in their homes; at the heart of these cribs are three figures: the newborn Jesus, Mary, and Joseph, her husband and the legal father of Jesus.

The sanctification of *time* goes together with the seven sacraments and the innumerable sacramentals that turn material signs into means for mediating the divine gifts. Such sanctification happens, of course, through the eucharistic celebration of the feasts and seasons of the liturgical year (above all, Advent, Christmas, Lent, and Easter). But time is also sanctified through the Liturgy of the Hours, when Catholics and other Christians gather at different hours of day or night in cathedrals, parish churches, monasteries, and other places to hear passages of scripture (and other sacred writings) being read and to sing or recite together psalms and further prayers. Those who follow the daily programme of official worship give praise to God, share in Christ's priestly office, and intercede for the salvation of the whole world. Vatican II's first document, *Sacrosanctum Concilium*, sets out beautifully how the divine office or Liturgy of the Hours sanctifies the passing of time on a daily and annual basis. Even casual visitors can sense how the singing of the divine office serves not only to worship God but also to make holy the daily flow of time.

Both/And

The first major section of this chapter has laid the ground for the second. It is typically Catholic to embrace 'both/and', and hold together things that some other Christians may tend to oppose to each other. Hence Catholics, like Orthodox Christians, do not accept an 'either/or' in the case of the sacraments and a broad range of sacramental practices that we have just summarized above. Sacramentals remain subordinate to baptism, the Eucharist, and the other five sacraments, but belong with them in consecrating to God through Christ the whole of bodily and human existence. There are numerous examples of the characteristically Catholic readiness to hold together, often in tension, things that others separate or even oppose.

Jesus and Mary

Like members of Orthodox Churches, Catholics do not accept an 'either/or' in the case of Jesus and his Mother. Many Protestant Reformers and their followers hold that honouring Mary (and, for that matter, other saints) somehow blurs the unique role of Jesus as Saviour. But Catholics do not admit a choice here; they want Jesus *and* his Mother. This instinct has prompted them into erecting in different parts of the world wayside scenes of Calvary. At the foot of the cross, Christ's Mother keeps her lonely vigil. Catholics feel very comfortable with images of Mary standing by her dying Son or holding her tiny baby in her arms.

Catholics, Orthodox, and some other Christians feel themselves understood and cherished by this woman and mother. A 4th-century Greek papyrus gives us in a Greek version the first

14. A modern Madonna and Child from Burma (Myanmar)

text of *Sub Tuum Presidium*, one of the oldest Christian prayers after those found in the Bible (e.g. the psalms in the Old Testament and the Lord's Prayer in the New Testament). It begins: 'Beneath your protective shelter we flee, holy Mother of God.' This prayer, in an expanded form, has continued to be used right down to the present day. Like the rosary with its joyful, sorrowful, and glorious mysteries – and, since 2002, mysteries of light – that commemorate the main stages in the story of Christ, the *Sub Tuum Presidium* moves from Mary to her Son: 'O glorious and blessed Virgin, our dear Lady, our mediator, our advocate, lead us to your Son, recommend us to your Son, present us to your Son.' Like this prayer, exquisite Marian antiphons (e.g. the *Salve Regina*), classical compositions for the *Magnificat* and *Ave Maria*, statues of Mary with her Son, stained-glass portrayals from medieval Europe, and Eastern icons from all centuries present Marian devotion at its best and truest. Mary's beauty, nobility, and importance are all derived through the Holy Spirit from her Son.

Both a 'vertical' and a 'horizontal' love

A Catholic 'both/and', shared by other Christians, concerns the love of God and love of one's neighbour. Catholics want to give time to God in prayer, either alone or with others, but they also want to care for all their neighbours in need. From the very beginning, a this-worldly and an other-worldly commitment have characterized Catholic Christianity. The ancient *Didache*, a text written probably around AD 90 and so one of the earliest Christian works outside the New Testament, enjoined not only the regular practice of daily prayer (8. 3) but also generous help towards those in need (4. 5–8).

Over the centuries, innumerable Catholic men and women have served others through schools, colleges, hospitals, and other social ministries (see Chapters 1 and 2). In this, they have been constantly supported by communities of men and women leading lives of silence and contemplative prayer.

In modern times, devotion to God in prayer and a practical love towards others have gone hand in hand for Catholic or Catholic-inspired groups that teach in a huge variety of educational institutions, provide health care of all kinds, run soup

15. Pope John Paul II embraces Mother Teresa of Calcutta after visiting one of her homes for the destitute, showing his deep regard for her holiness

kitchens, staff leprosaria, provide dying derelicts with care and dignified shelter, create homes for the mentally disabled, and assist and defend refugees and asylum-seekers.

Such engagement with and for the world happens with significantly different emphases. Justice and Peace groups, members of Opus Dei, those who support CAFOD (the Catholic Agency for Overseas Development), the Focolare Movement,

members of Christian Life Communities, lay affiliates of
Carmelites and Dominicans, and other movements work, think,
and pray in diverse ways. They do not live their Catholic vocation
in exactly the same way. But they are all concerned to be both
engaged with a suffering world and assiduous about communion
with God through prayer.

Faith and reason

Catholicism has never embraced the opposition between Athens
(standing for reason) and Jerusalem (standing for faith),
classically expressed by Tertullian (d. around AD 225) when he
denounced Greek philosophers and the heirs of Plato's Academy:
'What has Athens to do with Jerusalem? What has the Academy to
do with the Church? What have heretics to do with Christians?'
(*De Praescriptione Haereticorum*, 7). Through the 4th-century
Cappadocians (St Basil of Caesarea, St Gregory of Nazianzus, St
Gregory of Nyssa, St Macrina the Younger), such medieval writers
as St Thomas Aquinas and Dante, and down to the 1998 encyclical
of John Paul II, *Fides et Ratio* ('Faith and reason'), Catholic
Christianity has never accepted a separation between God's gift of
faith and the cultivation of human reason.

The Cappadocians and other fathers of the Church had received
an excellent education in the classics of Greek and Latin literature.
When barbarian invasions tore Europe apart, monasteries of men
and women in Ireland and elsewhere kept learning alive. We can
recall, for example, Rosvitha, a 10th-century canoness of an abbey
in Saxony. She was not only very learned in the scriptures, the
writings of the fathers of the Church, and classical Latin literature,
but also composed in Latin a number of plays and poems. By
leading a renewal in theological learning and recovering (through
Islamic and Jewish scholarship) the philosophy of Aristotle,
Aquinas expressed for all time a harmony between faith and
reason. Following his lead, Dante blended human learning and
divine revelation in the *Comedy*. His two companions in that

masterpiece were Virgil and his beloved Beatrice, the former symbolizing true humanism and the latter divine wisdom.

Occasionally, tensions grew between faith and reason or between the truths of revelation and worldly learning, above all after the rise of the natural sciences. Sometimes these conflicts arose from rational, scientific, and materialist claims to enjoy total authority over the interpretation and even the control of all reality. Sometimes Catholics, in particular Church officials, were to blame. After making the right decision to reform in 1582 the calendar of Julius Caesar, Roman authorities proved disastrously intransigent in the case of Galileo Galilei (1564–1642). Since his observations that the earth moved around the sun seemed to challenge the Church's authority to interpret the scriptures, he was forced to retract his position. His case came to symbolize for many people an antagonism between scientific reason and faith. But all truth is based in God, and there can never be final opposition between religious and scientific truths. The Austrian abbot Johann Gregor Mendel, through his experiments with peas in the monastery garden that prefigured modern genetics, in his own way symbolizes what Aquinas stood for: the basic harmony of all truth, whether known through divine revelation or human research.

That said, advances in the life sciences and technology need to be evaluated ethically and religiously; otherwise, they can threaten the dignity, environment, and even survival of the human race. With various governments increasingly ready to legalize experiments with human embryos, full and genuine dialogue between faith and scientific reason is more urgent than ever. In one of his novels, H. G. Wells (1866–1946) expressed this need by having a scientist (Dr Moreau) declare: 'I went on with this research just the way it led me … I have never troubled [myself] about the ethics of the matter' (*The Island of Dr Moreau*). Wells, for all his liberal ideas, recognized the danger of modern science refusing to be guided by moral norms.

Further both/ands

One can pile up a long list of further both/ands that typify
Catholicism: for example, both Eastern and Western ways of
worship; both a cross on the tower of a church and a crucifix
behind the altar; both married and celibate priests (the first being
typically the case in Eastern Catholicism and the second in
Western Catholicism); both bishops who come largely from the
diocesan clergy (the West) and bishops who come from monastic
life (the East); both the (very many) lay members and the
(comparatively few) ordained ministers; both saints and sinners
who belong to the same Church; both institutional structures and
charismatic initiatives; both prayerful fasting during Lent and
joyful feasting at Easter.

The same both/and attitude applies or, at least, should apply to the
differing tendencies and methods that characterize theology: an
emphasis on truth and intellectual rigour; an emphasis on
worship and beauty; and an emphasis on action for justice. One
might express this diversity by speaking of theologies of the head,
the heart, and the hands, respectively. The first style characterizes
much of European and North American theology; the second
describes the theology of Eastern Catholics and other Christians;
the third distinguishes liberation theology and its offshoots. A
truly Catholic view of theology should be open to all three
approaches.

The same kind of Catholic openness should typify attitudes
towards art, architecture, and music. Catholics need both the
medieval windows of Chartres Cathedral and the innovative,
Chinese-style windows of the restored cathedral in Shanghai. They
need both the glorious heritage of plainchant and tasteful modern
hymns.

With all these and other 'both/ands', can Catholics ever find
themselves confronted with a choice? At times there will obviously
be choices to make on practical issues, such as the time dedicated

to prayer and the time dedicated to helping those in distress. At other times, a particular 'both/and' could involve a choice between a true development or a false corruption. Nevertheless, it would bring an impoverished Catholic vision to exclude systematically one or other of the elements in the 'both/ands' listed above.

Unity

From the time of Ignatius of Antioch (d. around 107), Cyprian of Carthage (d. 258), and Augustine of Hippo (d. 430), we find Catholic Christians shrinking from divisions and sharing a gut feeling that worldwide unity must be maintained. Inevitable and, one should add, healthy tensions have continued to arise between unity and diversity, and between the inherited institutions (essentially the pastoral government of bishops in communion with the Bishop of Rome) and fresh movements inspired by the Holy Spirit that can bring beneficial developments in the life of the Church. Such situations are properly handled neither by an inflexible rigidity nor by a naive readiness to embrace every change. The Church at large constantly needs to apply the tests proposed by John Henry Newman (1801–90) and distinguish between faithful, life-giving developments and disloyal corruption.

In a world that now includes over 20,000 separate Christian denominations, Catholics hope that new movements, led by Spirit-filled and Spirit-guided men and women, should not bring separation and any breaking of communion with others. Rather, they should enrich the whole Church, whether these movements last for only a short time or for many centuries, as was the case with the religious families founded by Benedict, Scholastica, Dominic, Francis, Clare, and Ignatius Loyola.

Undoubtedly, the institutional authority of bishops has at times been exercised foolishly and sinfully against men and women who charismatically proposed fresh ideas and new commitments. But that same authority has often worked to defend and promote people raised by the Holy Spirit to minister to others in times of crisis and challenge.

The Second Vatican Council (*Gaudium et Spes*, 92) followed Pope John XXIII in endorsing the wise counsel of St Augustine of Hippo (d. 430): 'let there be unity in what is necessary, freedom in what is doubtful, and charity in everything (*sit in necessariis unitas, in dubiis libertas, in omnibus caritas*)'. This brings us to the agenda for the closing chapter, which will set out some of the major challenges facing the Catholic Church at the start of the third millennium.

Chapter 7
The future of Catholicism

My first six chapters, by setting themselves to describe the Catholic tradition, attended largely to the past and present state of Catholicism. But, in the aftermath of the over-centralized governance of John Paul II, the persistent controversies over changes in the liturgy, and the child abuse scandals that afflicted Catholicism in Australia, Ireland, the United Kingdom, and the USA, what concerns and dreams do I have about the future of the Catholic Church?

The future of humanity

The future of Catholicism is clearly bound up with the ecological, political, and social challenges that face the whole human race: global warming, the savagery of war, and religious and ideological differences threaten the survival of humanity.

Global warming

The Catholic tradition can draw on powerful resources to encourage a simpler lifestyle and discourage allowing our individual and collective existence to be driven by motives of immediate profit and security, or – putting it more bluntly – to be dominated by destructive fear and greed. The tradition launched by St Benedict and St Scholastica cared for the earth and fostered agricultural customs that respected the local eco-cycle. St Francis and St Clare praised God as revealed in creation and expressed love for all creatures. They continue to inspire many Christians (and others) to accept the call, found in the Genesis story of creation, and become responsible stewards of the created world and stop exploiting and destroying it at will. A satisfactory, or even possible, existence for future generations depends upon the present generation caring conscientiously for the planet, its living species, and the raw materials and sources of energy it provides.

Catholics, along with other Christians and those of other faiths, have the imperative role of persuading human beings and their leaders that the purpose of existence goes beyond mere material gratification and self-advancement. In far too many countries, a possessive individualism has weakened a sense of community and a shared commitment to the common good of present and future generations. Believers must do much more to encourage everyone to face the question: What life for the human family and its planet is truly worth defending and maintaining?

War

Chapter 5 recalled the desire of the Second Vatican Council to foster peace and establish an effective community of nations. John Paul II repeatedly spoke out against war and expressed his conviction that war never resolves conflicts among peoples. Right through his long pontificate (1978–2005), he followed the lead of Pope Paul VI by urging the principles of international law, the removal of injustices that provoke conflicts, and effective economic aid toward development, 'the new name for peace'. In his teaching and personal witness, John Paul II stressed the need for forgiveness between nations and all groups at odds with each other. As he put it in his message for the World Day of Peace in 2002, 'no peace without justice. No justice without forgiveness.' One might rephrase this message: 'if you seek peace, work for justice and forgiveness'.

Ideological differences

In that same peace message, John Paul II once again emphasized the urgent need for greater inter-faith understanding and cooperation. Worn out with age, gunshot wounds, and sickness, he gave right to the end a shining example by encouraging greater respect and solidarity between all religions. It was precisely his faith in the powerful presence of the risen Christ and of the Holy Spirit in all cultures and religions that supported such openness.

But contacts with 'others' at the highest level in the Catholic Church cannot suffice to achieve inter-faith harmony. Nor will dialogues between official representatives of different religions be enough to improve relations. Such dialogues will persist in being merely talk-shops, unless a loving readiness to hear and understand the 'other' becomes part of Catholic life at home, in the parishes, in schools, and at the workplace.

Any inter-religious dialogue and collaboration remains, however, hampered by the divisions between Christians. To the degree that Christians continue to be separated and at odds with each other, they are weakened in what they can do towards inter-faith relations. Undoubtedly, the ecumenical movement has succeeded to some extent intellectually, as patient Catholic exchanges with Anglicans, Lutherans, Methodists, and other Christians have uncovered a remarkable amount of common ground. But institutionally the goal of Christian unity remains a matter of hope and prayer.

Within the Catholic Church

Among the most urgent challenges within Catholicism itself, one can name: holding together the claims of unity and diversity; allowing much more room for the ministry of all the baptized; and encouraging everywhere a radical conversion to Jesus Christ.

Unity and diversity

At Vatican I, a centralized papacy was formalized; Vatican II
went on to spell out the unity and equality of all bishops who
form together a college of pastors 'with Peter and under Peter'
(Chapter 4 above). There is need for a central authority, but this
authority should be exercised in ways that are compatible with the
rights and requirements of particular churches and particular
cultures. Around the world, Catholic churches and other buildings
normally display photographs of the current pope and the local
bishop. Even more importantly, the Eucharistic Prayer remembers
by name those two leaders. Both practices hint at the desire to
honour both local diversity and worldwide unity, so as to further a
healthily operating communion between the Bishop of Rome and
the bishops of particular churches.

Early in the 20th century, many Catholics welcomed a new era
encouraged by Pope Pius XI, when in the so-called 'mission
countries' local priests, instead of foreign missionaries, became the
bishops. 'Rome rule means home rule', they announced proudly.
Today the bishops around the world are generally natives of their
own countries. Yet home rule is at times spoiled by Rome rule.
Instead of being the last court of appeal, some officials of the

16. Benedict XVI, elected Pope in April 2005

Roman Curia claim to be the 'judges' in the first instance. They want to maintain good order and Catholic unity (or is it sometimes a false and even inflexible uniformity?) by exercising centralized power over particular churches.

Subsidiarity, or not taking to the higher level matters that can and should be dealt with at a lower, local level, clearly constitutes a healthy principle for life together, both in society at large and in the Catholic Church in particular. But some Vatican officials do not always honour the principle in practice and occasionally question it in theory.

Ministry for all the baptized

St Paul pointed out how being baptized into Christ implies overcoming religious, social, and gender barriers: 'There is no longer Jew or Greek, there is no longer slave or free, there is no longer male and female; for you are all one in Christ Jesus' (Gal. 3: 28). Paul himself struggled to break down the barriers between Jews and Gentiles. When the slave Onesimus ran away, the apostle pleaded with the owner (Philemon) to receive the slave back as a brother and gently suggested that Philemon set him free. The last chapter of the Letter to the Romans shows how much Paul valued the ministry of women such as Prisca (Priscilla). There is obviously much unfinished business in overcoming the barriers between Jews and Gentiles, in delivering from oppression those who suffer under different forms of slavery, and in establishing a true equality for women in the Church and in society at large.

All the baptized, men and women alike, are responsible for the life and mission of the Church. Every parish draws life and strength not only from the pastor but also from lay men and lay women and their ministries as lectors, acolytes, Eucharistic ministers, and the rest. Every one of the baptized belongs fully to the Church, shares in the priestly, prophetic, and kingly mission of Christ, and offers, or should offer, their unique contribution to the well-being and growth of the whole community.

17. A christening in Brixton, London. The water of baptism brings new life, and the Easter candle symbolizes the light of Jesus who will guide the baptized

For a long time in many parts of the world (notably in Latin America), the Catholic faithful have lacked a sufficient number of priests and can attend the Eucharist only every few months, if that. Increasingly in the United States, thousands of parishes do not have a resident priest. Many of these parishes have been entrusted to the pastoral care of women religious, some to permanent deacons, and a few to lay persons. This worldwide situation raises two questions: Should the female parish administrators be ordained permanent deacons? Should male permanent deacons, many of whom are married, be invited to accept ordination to the priesthood?

Many countries have long suffered from a chronic lack of priests. In other countries, which used to have sufficient priests to staff the parishes, numbers of priests are steadily declining. The celebration of the Eucharist is the heart of the life of the Catholic Church. But far too many Catholics are unable, Sunday by Sunday, to share in the Eucharist, find in it the centre of their existence, and draw from it the strength they require for their lives. To meet the challenge, we need the farsighted policy of ordaining to the priesthood married men, who in many cases are already exercising pastoral leadership as catechists, pastoral administrators, or permanent deacons.

Radical conversion to Christ

In the Western world and elsewhere, millions of Catholics have disengaged themselves and no longer share in the Eucharist. They have been alienated from the Church by poor homilies, liturgies that no longer engage them, and other defective features of Catholic life and worship. For their sake and for the sake of the world at large, the whole Catholic Church needs a radical conversion to the living Christ. His presence can enable Catholics not only to renew their fellowship in the life of the Church but also to work for the good of all human beings and to bring to a disenchanted and suffering world the good news that is Jesus himself. More than ever, humanity needs Catholics and other Christians whose lives are totally centred on Jesus. Without such a conversion, any reforms in the Catholic Church will remain at best merely cosmetic decoration. By sharing through Christ ever so much more in the ecstasy of love that is the life of the tripersonal God, the Church will be enabled to bring to the whole world the faith, justice, and peace that it so urgently requires.

In the third millennium, the human family finds its future existence under threat. More than ever it needs the message of Christ who is the Light of the whole world. He is the full and final key to what human life is ultimately about, the One who brings life in abundance. My dream is that, through a deep conversion to Jesus, more and more Catholics and other Christians may embody and convey his role in uniting human beings with God and with one another. May their way of life more and more form a unified community that signals and mediates the presence and significance of Jesus Christ for all human beings in their relationship with God and with one another. In his homily at the inaugural Mass of 24 April 2005, Pope Benedict XVI took up his ministry as successor of Peter very much in terms of turning to Christ: 'If we let Christ into our lives, we lose nothing, nothing, absolutely nothing of what makes life free, beautiful, and great.' The Pope ended his homily with words that echoed John Paul II and sum up the central message of Catholicism: 'Open wide the doors to Christ, and you will find true life.'

Further reading

Sources

St Thomas Aquinas, *Summa Theologiae*, tr. T. Gilby *et al.*, 60 vols (London: Eyre & Spottiswoode, 1964–6).

David B. Barrett *et al.*, *World Christian Encyclopedia*, 2 vols, 2nd edn. (New York: Oxford University Press, 2001).

Wolfgang Beinert and Francis Schüssler Fiorenza (eds), *Handbook of Catholic Theology* (New York: Crossroad, 1995).

Thomas S. Bokenkotter, *Concise History of the Catholic Church* (New York: Doubleday, 1990).

James Buckley *et al.* (eds), *The Blackwell Companion to Catholicism* (Oxford: Blackwell, 2007).

Catechism of the Catholic Church (Vatican City: Libreria Editrice Vaticana, 1992; various editions of the English translation).

F. L. Cross and E. A. Livingstone (eds), *The Oxford Dictionary of the Christian Church*, 4th edn. (Oxford: Oxford University Press, 2006).

Heinrich Denzinger and Peter Hünermann, *Enchiridion Symbolorum, Definitionum et Declarationum*, 17th edn. (Freiburg im Breisgau: Herder, 1991).

Erwin Fahlbusch *et al.*, *The Encyclopedia of Christianity* (Grand Rapids, Mich.: Eerdmans, 1998–).

Austin Flannery (ed.), *Vatican Council II: The Conciliar and Post Conciliar Documents*, revised edn. (Northport, NY: Costello, 1996).

Hubert Jedin and J. Dolan (eds), *History of the Church*, 10 vols (New York: Crossroad, 1981–2).

Philippe Levillain (ed.), *The Papacy: An Encyclopedia*, 3 vols (London: Routledge, 2003).

Josef Neuner and Jacques Dupuis (eds), *The Christian Faith*, 7th edn. (Bangalore/New York: Theological Publications in India/Alba House, 2001).

New Catholic Encyclopedia, 15 vols, 2nd edn. (Washington, DC: Catholic University of America, 2003).

Ken Parrry (ed.), *The Blackwell Dictionary of Eastern Christianity* (Oxford: Blackwell, 1999).

Ken Parry (ed.), *The Blackwell Companion to Eastern Christianity* (Oxford: Blackwell, 2007).

Karl Rahner, *Theological Investigations*, 23 vols (London: Darton, Longman & Todd, 1961–92).

Ronald Roberson, *Eastern Christian Churches*, 6th edn. (Rome: Pontifical Oriental Institute, 1999).

Norman Tanner (ed.), *Decrees of the Ecumenical Councils*, 2 vols (London: Sheed and Ward, 1990).

General

Karl Adam, *The Spirit of Catholicism* (London: Sheed and Ward, 1929).

Daniel Donovan, *Distinctively Catholic* (Mahwah, NJ: Paulist Press, 1997).

Dante Alighieri, *The Divine Comedy*, tr. Robin Kirkpatrick, 3 vols (London: Penguin, 2006–7).

Eamon Duffy, *Faith of Our Fathers: Reflections on Catholic Tradition* (London: Continuum, 2004).

Thomas H. Groome, *What Makes Us Catholic: Eight Gifts for Life* (San Francisco: Harper San Francisco, 2002).

Darrell Jodock (ed.), *Catholicism Contending with Modernity* (Cambridge: Cambridge University Press, 2000).

Henri de Lubac, *Catholicism: Christ and the Common Destiny of Man* (San Francisco: Ignatius Press, 1988).

Richard P. McBrien, *Catholicism*, 2nd edn. (San Francisco: Harper San Francisco, 1994).

Gerald O'Collins, *Living Vatican II: The 21st Council for the 21st Century* (Mahwah, NJ: Paulist Press, 2006).

Gerald O'Collins and Mario Farrugia, *Catholicism: The Story of Catholic Christianity* (Oxford: Oxford University Press, 2003).

Joseph Ratzinger, *Introduction to Christianity* (New York: Herder & Herder, 1969).

Roderick Strange, *The Catholic Faith* (London: Darton, Longman & Todd, 2001).

Roderick Strange, *Living Catholicism* (London: Darton, Longman & Todd, 2001).

Chapter 1

Peter Brown, *The Rise of Western Christendom: Triumph and Diversity AD 200–1000* (Oxford: Blackwell, 1996).

Henry Chadwick, *The Church in Ancient Society: From Galilee to Gregory the Great* (Oxford: Clarendon Press, 2001).

Eamon Duffy, *Saints and Sinners: A History of the Popes* (New Haven, Conn.: Yale University Press, 1997).

Adrian Hastings (ed.), *A World History of Christianity* (London: Cassell, 1999).

Zachary Karabell, *People of the Book: The Forgotten History of Islam and the West* (London: John Murray, 2007).

Edward Norman, *The Roman Catholic Church: An Illustrated History* (London: Thames and Hudson, 2007).

O'Collins and Farrugia, *Catholicism*, pp. 1–76.

Elizabeth Rees, *Celtic Saints: Passionate Wanderers* (London: Thames and Hudson, 2000).

Francis A. Sullivan, *From Apostles to Bishops* (Mahwah, NJ: Paulist Press, 2001).

Margaret Visser, *The Geometry of Love* (New York: Farrar, Straus & Giroux, 2000).

Diana Webb, *Pilgrims and Pilgrimages in the Medieval West* (London: Tauris, 1999).

Chapter 2

Giuseppe Alberigo and Joseph A. Komonchak, *History of Vatican II*, 5 vols (Maryknoll, NY: Orbis, 1996–2006).

Robert Bireley, *The Refashioning of Catholicism 1450–1700* (Basingstoke: Macmillan, 1999).

Owen Chadwick, *Britian and the Vatican during the Second World War* (Cambridge: Cambridge University Press, 1986).

David G. Dalin, *The Myth of Hitler's Pope* (Washington, DC: Regnery, 2005).

Silvia Evangelisti, *A History of Convent Life 1450–1700* (Oxford: Oxford University Press, 2007).

Adrian Hastings, *The Church in Africa 1450–1950* (Oxford: Oxford University Press, 1994).

Hans J. Hillerbrand (ed.), *The Oxford Encyclopedia of the Reformation*, 4 vols (Oxford: Oxford University Press, 1996).

O'Collins and Farrugia, *Catholicism*, pp. 76–95.

Ronald J. Rychlak, *Hitler, the War, and the Pope* (Huntington, Ind.: Our Sunday Visitor, 2000).

Charles Taylor, *A Secular Age* (Cambridge, Mass.: Harvard University Press, 2007).

Thomas Worcester (ed.), *The Cambridge Companion to the Jesuits* (Camhridge: Cambridge University Press, 2008).

Chapter 3

Lewis Ayres, *Nicaea and its Legacy* (Oxford: Oxford University Press, 2004).

Pontifical Biblical Commission, *The Interpretation of the Bible in the Church* (Vatican City: Libreria Editrice Vaticana, 1993).

Stanley M. Burgess, *The Holy Spirit: Medieval Roman Catholic and Reformation Traditions* (Peabody, Mass.: Hendrickson, 1997).

Yves Congar, *I Believe in the Holy Spirit*, 3 vols (London: Geoffrey Chapman, 1983).

Stephen Davis *et al.* (eds), *The Trinity* (Oxford: Oxford University Press, 1999).

Stephen Davis *et al.* (eds), *The Incarnation* (Oxford: Oxford University Press, 2001).

Gerald O'Collins, *Jesus Our Redeemer: A Christian Approach to Salvation* (Oxford: Oxford University Press, 2007).

O'Collins and Farrugia, *Catholicism*, pp. 96–233.

Chapter 4

Raymond E. Brown *et al.* (eds), *Peter in the New Testament* (New York: Paulist Press, 1993).

Louis-Marie Chauvet, *The Sacraments* (Collegeville, Minn.: Liturgical Press, 2001).

David M. Coffey, *The Sacrament of Reconciliation* (Collegeville, Minn.: Liturgical Press, 2001).

Avery Dulles, *Models of the Church*, 2nd edn. (Maryknoll, NY: Orbis, 1992).

Maxwell E. Johnson, *The Rites of Christian Initiation: Their Evolution and Interpretation* (Collegeville, Minn.: Liturgical Press, 1999).

James Martin (ed.), *Celebrating Good Liturgy: A Guide to the Ministries of the Mass* (Chicago: Loyola Press, 2005).

Enrico Massa, *The Celebration of the Eucharist: The Origin of the Rite and the Development of Its Interpretation* (Collegeville, Minn.: Pueblo, 1999).

O'Collins and Farrugia, *Catholicism*, pp. 234–334.

Peter C. Phan (ed.), *The Gift of the Church: A Textbook on Ecclesiology in Honor of Patrick Granfield, O.S.B.* (Collegeville, Minn.: Liturgical Press, 2000).

Thomas J. Reese, *Inside the Vatican: The Politics and Organization of the Catholic Church* (Cambridge, Mass.: Harvard University Press, 1996).

K. Schatz, *Papal Primacy from Its Origins to the Present* (Collegeville, Minn.: Liturgical Press, 1996).

Chapter 5

John Mahoney, *The Making of Moral Theology: A Study of the Roman Catholic Tradition* (Oxford: Clarendon Press, 1989).

John T. Noonan, Jr, *A Church That Can and Cannot Change: The Development of Catholic Moral Teaching* (Notre Dame, Ind.: University of Notre Dame Press, 2005).

O'Collins and Farrugia, *Catholicism*, pp. 335–66.

Walter J. Woods, *Walking with Faith: New Perspectives on the Sources and Shaping of Catholic Moral Life* (Collegeville, Minn.: Michael Glazier, 1998).

Chapter 6

Thomas Bamat and Jean-Paul Wiest (eds), *Popular Catholicism in a World Church: Seven Case Studies in Inculturation* (Maryknoll, NY: Orbis, 1999).

Sarah Jane Boss (ed.), *Mary: The Complete Resource* (London: Continuum, 2007).

Caroline H. Ebertshäuser *et al.* (eds), *Mary: Art, Culture, and Religion through the Ages* (New York: Crossroad, 1998).

Elizabeth Kuhn, *The Habit: A History of the Clothing of Catholic Nuns* (New York: Doubleday, 2003).

Peter Lynch, *The Church's Story: A History of Pastoral Care and Vision* (London: St Paul's Publications, 2005).

John Henry Newman, *An Essay on the Development of Christian Doctrine* (Harmondsworth: Penguin, 1974).

O'Collins and Farrugia, *Catholicism*, pp. 367–80.

Michael Walsh, *Dictionary of Catholic Devotions* (San Francisco: Harper San Francisco, 1993).

Chapter 7

Drew Christiansen and Walter Grazer (eds), *'And God Saw That It Was Good': Catholic Theology and the Environment* (Washington, DC: United States Catholic Conference, 1996).

Catherine E. Clifford, *The Groupe des Dombes: A Dialogue of Conversion* (New York: Peter Lang, 2005).

William D'Antonio and Anthony Pogorelc (eds), *Voices of the Faithful: Loyal Catholics Striving for Change* (New York: Herder & Herder, 2007).

Jacques Dupuis, *Christianity and the Religions* (Maryknoll, NY: Orbis, 2002).

Umberto Eco and Carlo Maria Martini, *Belief or Unbelief?* (New York: Arcade Publishing, 2000).

Philip Jenkins, *The Next Christendom: The Coming of Global Christianity*, 2nd edn. (Oxford: Oxford University Press, 2007).

Piero Marini, *A Challenging Reform: Realizing the Vision of Liturgical Renewal* (Dublin: Columba Press, 2007).

Paul Murray (ed.), *Receptive Ecumenism and the Call to Catholic Learning: Exploring a Way for Contemporary Ecumenism* (Oxford: Oxford University Press, 2007).

Gerald O'Collins, *Living Vatican II*, pp. 147–70.

Gerald O'Collins, *Salvation For All: God's Other Peoples* (Oxford: Oxford University Press, 2008).

John Quinn, *The Reform of the Papacy* (New York: Crossroad, 1999).

Edward Stourton, *John Paul II: Man of History* (London: Hodder & Stoughton, 2006).

Timeline

c. 30	Death and resurrection of Jesus and the first Pentecost
c. 36	Calling of St Paul
c. 67	Martyrdom of Sts Peter and Paul in Rome
70	Destruction of Jerusalem
c. 200	Death of St Irenaeus of Lyons
313	Edict of Milan and freedom for Christians
325	First Council of Nicaea
381	First Council of Constantinople
430	Death of St Augustine of Hippo
431	Council of Ephesus
451	Council of Chalcedon
c. 461	Death of St Patrick
c. 523	Death of St Brigid
c. 530	Death of St Benedict
c. 543	Death of St Scholastica
590–604	Papacy of St Gregory the Great
632	Death of Muhammad
800	Charlemagne crowned in Rome
1054	Catholics and Orthodox excommunicate each other
1073–85	Papacy of Gregory VII
1095	Pope Urban II launches first Crusade

1221	Death of St Dominic
1226	Death of St Francis of Assisi
1253	Death of St Clare
1321	Death of Dante Alighieri
1450	Johannes Gutenberg creates the printing press
1492	Christopher Columbus discovers America
1517	Martin Luther publishes his 95 theses
1545–63	Council of Trent
1556	Death of St Ignatius Loyola
1582	Death of St Teresa of Avila
1640	Death of Matteo Ricci in Beijing
1704	Pope Clement XI condemns 'Chinese Rites'
1776	American Declaration of Independence
1789	Start of French Revolution
1815	Death of Archbishop John Carroll
1846–78	Papacy of Blessed Pius IX
1869/70	First Vatican Council
1890	Death of Cardinal John Henry Newman
1914–18	First World War
1939–45	Second World War
1958–63	Papacy of Blessed John XXIII
1962–5	Second Vatican Council
1963–78	Papacy of Paul VI
1978–2005	Papacy of John Paul II
April 2005	Benedict XVI elected pope

Index